AF368859

MY BABY'S FIRST YEAR

NICOLE ANIDJAR

www.baby.justknowbooks.com

EDITATUM

Interior layout: © Editatum
Translation: © Emily McPeek

First edition: may 2020

ISBN: 978-84-18121-29-6
Legal deposit: M-12642-2020

PRINTED IN SPAIN

Acknowledgements

I would like to thank my parents in principle because as I get deeper into the world of parenting I realize what a great effort they made (and continue to make) to form me into the person I am today.

To my children who, like good teachers, have challenged me, taught me, made me grow and surpass myself, all this while showing me how deep love is and how much fun life can be.

To my husband, my faithful companion for being an accomplice to my madness, for supporting me, not only with these new parenting schemes, but with this wonderful project called Mama Nicole and Informed Parenting and for believing in me more than I believe in myself. Without it, none of this would be possible.

To Erika, one of my great teachers in breastfeeding and parenting, for being a personal and professional reference and who has made me a mother and student with tools to achieve a light and enjoyable motherhood.

To the team at Editatum for believing in me and encouraging me to write this book that has become my third baby.

And finally, but surely not least, to all those mothers, and some fathers too, who accompany me day by day in this important work of raising and who place their trust in me by asking me questions that have allowed me to investigate, learn and question what I thought I knew, leading me to grow more and more every day and to want to learn more. Without you, my work would be meaningless.

About the author

Nicole Anidjar, better known as Mama Nicole, Dentist, Breastfeeding Specialist, Parenting Consultant and creator of Informed Parenting.

A mother and professional with a clear goal: to make mothers enjoy raising their children to the fullest through empowerment and security.

Passionate about the world of motherhood, she has completed her Specialization in Human Lactation at the Center for Breastfeeding Studies and since 2016 has worked with mothers on a daily basis in their desire to breastfeed and to have a more conscious upbringing. She has been trained in infant feeding, motor development of children from 0 to 2 years old, respectful upbringing, positive discipline, as well as studying pedagogical philosophies such as the Montessori method. She is in the process of becoming an Expert in Accompanying Conscious Motherhood and Respectful Parenting from the Psychology and Parenting School.

As a result of her personal and professional experience, she created the Informed Parenting philosophy that aims to help mothers empower themselves and make conscious decisions that result in greater parental satisfaction and therefore healthier and happier families.

Index

Introduction 15

Pregnancy and Childbirth 19

The First Three Months 33

Three to six months 59

Six Months 87

Eight to Twelve Months 117

Twelve Months 131

Epilogue 133

If I were pregnant again, even knowing everything I know so far, I would read this book,

The reasons? A human, objective, transcendent and researched vision of the baby's first year and also of the most frequent concerns we have as mothers.

The concept of Informed Parenting raised by Mama Nicole is relevant and useful for any mother looking for a word of encouragement and the power of information.

This outline of breastfeeding and parenting, which is passed on from quarter to quarter due to the most important changes in the baby, collaborates with making decisions that are tailored to the knowledge of each stage of development.

This material is even more valuable because it has been developed through the experiences of not one but two children, the experience of living in a country in turmoil and then migration.

Convinced that it will be a special contribution to those who acquire it, I am left with an excellent taste in my mouth when I see information with scientific evidence, my own experience and experience with other mothers captured in such a simple and digestible way.

Definitely a book that every pregnant woman and mother should have.

Erika Urbáez Aguilera

Breastfeeding Specialist
Respectful Parenting Consultant

Introduction

Informed Childrearing

The story of Informed Childrearing, and how I arrived at this work of empowerment and guidance in motherhood, begins with a mom who "leapt" into it without truly understanding the important role she was about to take on. That was me in my first pregnancy.

With my first baby, I was completely lost. I didn't think I needed to study or get informed because "there's no manual on raising a child, right?" I became a mother without knowing anything about newborns, the process of childbirth, breastfeeding and other forms of nutrition, or anything else that would come later. I dove into motherhood blindly assuming that everything would turn out fine because nobody really decides to do something believing that it might not go the way they expect.

Challenges are an inherent part of motherhood. We all, at some point, have to face some obstacle, and clearly I was not immune to that. As I'll tell you later on, childbirth as a starting point for motherhood was not a positive experience for me, and it left me feeling insecure, uncomfortable and afraid of what was to come. And then nursing... Like many mothers, I was met with an unexpected reality: breastfeeding wasn't "natural", or easy, or instinctive, it was a complete disaster.

I spent weeks suffering physical and emotional pain and didn't have anyone who really understood me. They said it was "normal", that that's just how it was in the first few weeks. Between the emotional scars from childbirth, the failed breastfeeding, the lack of sleep, the fear, the insecurity, and, of course, the commentary from other people, I was on the brink of insanity. Until I reached a point where I said to myself, "Being a mom can't be this awful," and I started to do research on breastfeeding, which was the most immediate problem I had.

I read, researched, had consultations with lactation specialists, and discovered that it was a world in itself. Finally, I solved my main problem with painful nursing, but guess what? After that came another pain of another nature that neither my pediatrician nor my gynecologist knew what to make of.

But this time, I was a different person. I had foundational information: the pain wasn't normal and there were, in fact, people who could help me. I didn't stress out, I didn't worry, I didn't get frustrated, or cry; I simply took care of the problem proactively and sought help where I knew I would get it, and I solved it almost immediately, with no hassle, with no suffering.

That's when I **understood**. I understood the wonderful power of having information. I understood that maternity is only terrible when we don't know anything, when we are unsure. When we expect something unrealistic, when we live a reality that we don't like, when we're afraid. And there's no better antidote for fear than information and empowerment. .

And that is how Informed Childrearing was conceived, without me even realizing it. My thirst for information and desire to support and empower other mothers led me to specialize in lactation and infant nutrition, to train in subjects related to raising children, and to grow along with my children, as a mother and as a companion for other mothers to be **happy in motherhood**.

The first year of your baby's life is full of changes and, therefore, challenges. I hope that this book, more than giving you answers, makes you ask questions and encourages you to explore the wonderful world of Informed Childrearing, where there are no set rules, only mothers who use their feminine wisdom to understand what is best for their families and then educate themselves so that they can raise their children accordingly.

So, I invite you to join me on this journey through the first year of a baby's life, to learn about the most common problems and what to do about them, to empower yourself and to become happy in motherhood.

I invite you to **enjoy the power of confident childrearing**.

With love,
Mama Nicole

Pregnancy and Childbirth

The Function of Pregnancy

Although the objective of this book is to talk about us and our babies in the first year after birth, I couldn't leave out such a decisive and profound time in motherhood as pregnancy and childbirth.

You become a mother from the moment you see the positive on the pregnancy test. Those little lines represent the "birth" of a new person: someone who will no longer be preoccupied with herself, so that she can genuinely preoccupy and occupy herself with another (or others). Where two or more souls live in a single body, making this a completely transformational period (physically, emotionally, spiritually, mentally... and, well, financially too 👶).

Pregnancy has many functions. Most of them, such as the growth of your baby, will unfold without you making the slightest effort. Another function is to give you a prudent amount of time to process the idea that you will be a mother and to prepare yourself for the arrival of your little one.But how do we actually prepare for this?

For some, like me in my first pregnancy, preparation consists of buying a thousand and one things that they tell us we have to buy, painting the nursery and putting away the clothes. Others, somewhat more judicious, understand that, to be a mother, you have to know things, and they start looking for information from the beginning of their pregnancy.

And yes, I applaud those mothers. Pregnancy is the exact and ideal moment to educate and prepare yourself for your role.

People study millions of things: marketing to increase sales in a company, engineering to build buildings, cooking to open a restaurant, but how is it that, sometimes, it doesn't even occur to us to study for the biggest company we'll have in our lives?

This is how, while your baby is developing, you should also develop your Informed Childrearing.

This philosophy, Informed Childrearing, which you will find throughout this entire book and which is a part of each one of my messages, has a clear goal: for every mother to enjoy motherhood. And that enjoyment depends on how confident we are about what we want and what we do.

Then, it comes like a wave of anxiety. You know you have to know things, but you don't know what you have to know in the first place (what a tongue-twister 😬). Well, I'm going to help you with that. You don't need to get overwhelmed by every detail of childrearing. At this point in your pregnancy, there's just one question you need to answer: **how do you want to feed your baby?**

Answering this question mindfully and knowledgeably will be your compass in the face of difficulties, the outline of your goal so that you know what actions to take in every situation. Not knowing what you want will only make you second-guess the different options without really believing in any of them.

Once you answer, the next step is to educate yourself. Many people are surprised to learn that, **while there is science behind breastfeeding, there is also science behind bottle feeding**. Either method, poorly understood, can lead to, shall we say, *complicated* results. There are many, many resources to empower yourself, such as books and lactation courses; find one that best suits you, and get informed (and, if necessary, I can help you with that through my online courses).

So, if you really want to be effective and take direct action in your **Informed Childrearing**, and, in so doing, enjoy your motherhood, define your goal now.

What type of food do you want to give your baby?

Our Starting Point in Motherhood
Childbirth

Let's be frank, giving birth isn't fun.

I have yet to meet a woman who is anxious to give birth or excited about labor per se. It's more like a moment of chaos, or a sort of "penitence" that we must overcome to get the grand prize: our baby. Between the insanity of the fact that a human being is literally coming out of you, all the changes that that means for your body, and, of course, the pain, giving birth is an experience that evokes apprehension and fear.

Having established that no one likes labor for labor's sake, I want to take some time to share with you my two birth stories, briefly, to better communicate my message on this topic.

With my first child, I was in such a state of terror that I couldn't even think about that moment without shaking. I didn't want to go to birthing classes, or get information. My plan was, "have them take the kid out" and get out of there as fast as possible.

That day, I hadn't yet felt the first contraction and I was already asking for anesthesia. **I said I didn't want to feel pain, but really I didn't even want to live that experience**. There was definitely something very, very wrong: **my attitude**. Life was presenting me (as it does to all women) with something I didn't like, something that made me disgusted, afraid, and how did I react? By using all of my energies to ignore it beforehand, and then, when the time came, it was exactly as bad as I had decided it would be. I didn't feel any of the contractions (I was anesthetized down to the last nerve), and just the same, the entire experience seemed horrible to me.

But how could I hope to experience it any other way, if I was already so committed? Then came post-partum... If giving birth was bad, that malaise was multiplied post-partum. Everything hurt, everything bothered me.

And that's how my motherhood began. Amidst complaints, discomfort, a negative attitude, and lots and lots of crying (on my part). You could say it was a "rough" start.

With my second baby, I was a new person already. Informed Childrearing had come into my life. Every step I took with my child was taken mindfully, and it was under that same premise that I decided to approach my second birth.

I began a process of exploring my emotions and my fears; I asked myself questions like, "What am I afraid of?" "Why am I afraid of that?" Later, I started to educate myself on childbirth and its physical and emotional implications, and what kinds of decisions I could make. I discovered the concept of a birth plan, and I created mine together with my husband.

I did everything the opposite of how I had in my first pregnancy. Before, I had tried to ignore anything that had to do with giving birth, at all costs; this time, I dove into the subject headfirst.

I decided that my attitude would be more positive. I accepted that pain was an inherent part of the process, which I still didn't like, but I was more focused on confronting it and not on trying to make it disappear.

My fears were still there, the uncertainty was the same, my rejection of pain had not lessened, but my attitude? It was completely different now.

After much reading and studying, I made the decision that I wanted to *try* to give birth without anesthesia. I, personally, felt that an epidural brought more risks than benefits.

What happened that day? I was equally terrified, really. I was very nervous to be giving birth again. *But I was at peace.* Long story short, yes, I gave birth without an epidural. It hurt, a lot, but every contraction, every push, was another battle in which I was victorious over my old self. As for post-partum, there was no comparing the second time with the first. Yes, there was discomfort, I was tired, but everything, in general, was better: I was happy, pleased, at peace with my body and with my experience.

How do you explain that, in one birth, where I didn't feel any contractions, the experience was so awful, and in another, where I felt every last second of pain, it was better? Easy—**my attitude.**

The reason I'm telling you all of this is that it is our starting point in motherhood. It's the first time we are "called upon" to face something that we don't like, and to do it positively.

 EYE!

Your attitude towards childbirth will largely determine your ability to tolerate difficulties in the future. There will always be things about being a mother that you don't like (sleepless nights, the demands of your children, the crying...). Giving birth is just the first of them, and, if you ask me, it isn't even the hardest.

Regardless of whether you use an epidural or not, whether you give birth vaginally or by cesarean, the idea is for you to make the birth your own, for you to make peace with the outcome of the experience no matter what. Keep in mind that things won't always go the way you expected: maybe you planned on having a natural birth and ultimately you have to have a C-section, there could be complications, the baby could have a problem during the birth... All of these are possible scenarios, which is why it's important for you to have positive energy.

In the face of obstacles, especially during childbirth, it's possible that the only thing under your control is your attitude, how you accept and confront whatever specific thing is happening.

I don't think it was a coincidence that it was hard for me to enjoy those first months with my first child. I was overwhelmed by taking care of him, I felt like I couldn't understand him, the late nights, the breastfeeding, everything was weighing on me. I believe I began my motherhood with a low—and I mean very low—tolerance for challenges, and that translated to everything stressing me out, starting with giving birth and continuing like that for months. Later, finally, I started a transformative personal process that allowed me to not only create and implement Informed Childrearing, but also share it.

Just as I changed my attitude and saw firsthand how motherhood became less burdensome and more enjoyable, so too I invite you to change and improve your own.

I'm sure that after reading this, you'll still be somewhat afraid of giving birth, but remember, an epidural won't take away your fear—information will. The more informed you are and the more positive your attitude, the better your starting point, childbirth, will be, and that will persist over time and in raising your child.

Their Staring Point in Life
Skin-to-Skin Contact

Regardless of whether you want to breastfeed or not, understanding **immediate/early skin-to-skin contact** will help you to set another standard in your motherhood and in how the beginning of your little one's life will develop.

Put yourself in your baby's shoes: they're in your belly in a state of absolute pleasure, at the perfect temperature, nothing to bother them, just the right amount of stimulus, eating whenever they want, never knowing an unpleasant sensation.

And suddenly, without warning, their reality changes and they enter a world which, at first, seems quite hostile. It's cold, it isn't contained, so they can't control their arms and legs, the light irritates them, the noise stuns them, they sense insecurity and an imminent threat.

And what happens next?

» **Option 1**: They are whisked away to be weighed, measured, vaccinated and washed, until finally, from exhaustion or resignation, the baby calms down and, hours later, makes contact with the only thing they know and want: their mother.

» **Option 2**: After just a few seconds of chaos and fear, they find what they most expect: you, their mom.

Body heat that soothes them, a scent and heartbeat that they recognize, and the opportunity to fulfill their genetic mission: latch onto your breast and say, "Okay, this isn't so bad... I'm going to be all right, my mom is here."

Which would you prefer? Which do you think is the best way to begin life?

Skin-to-skin contact (SSC), apart from being the most logical transition from the uterus to the world, is a practice that offers many physical, nutritional and psychological benefits, which I've shared below:

» Colonization with bacteria from the mother, strengthening the baby's immature immune system.

» Reduced crying time for the child, and, consequently, less stress.

» Improved blood sugar levels.

» A body temperature one degree higher than babies in incubators.

» Improved oxygen saturation.

» Greater cardiorespiratory stability.

» Less pain due to breast engorgement in mothers.

» Lower levels of anxiety for mothers.

» High concentration of oxytocin, which improves the flow of colostrum, keeps the mother happy, and causes the uterus to contract, preventing hemorrhaging.

» Greater confidence for the mother with regard to breastfeeding.

» Longer nursing period.

» **In babies with SSC, latching onto the mother's breast is done in a correct position in 86% of cases, while this only occurs in 20.5% of cases with separated infants.**

» Beneficial effects in the bonding process.

But besides that, and this is really what I want to focus on, skin-to-skin contact makes us feel like better mothers, which then makes us *be* better mothers. How does that work? I'll explain: early SSC triggers the release of a hormone called oxytocin, the love hormone. Its levels explode the instant we feel our baby's tiny body so close to ours, and it basically gets us "high" on love, predisposing us to happiness.

A study was done on the relationship between skin-to-skin contact and maternal satisfaction, and I'd like to quote part of their results.

The duration of the early contact is significantly associated with a higher degree of maternal satisfaction, with high rates of maternal behaviors of interaction with the infants seen during contact. Likewise, mothers observe adaptation or approximation behaviors in their babies with greater frequency the longer the contact period is.

Matronas Profesión 2004; vol. 5 (15): 12-18

The ways in which immediate SSC influences motherhood go beyond the physical benefits (which are many). It is also related to our starting point in childrearing in terms of **how we feel as mothers** from that first moment. It is a way to stop feeling confused, afraid, or insecure so that we can *simply feel satisfied.*

So, what should I do? How does it work?

It's so simple: just let yourself go. Ideally, once your baby comes out (whether via cesarean or vaginal birth), they will put him (or her) onto your body. Without bathing the baby, or you, and without any material coming between the two of you. Leaving the baby's hands uncovered will allow the process to flow better. And that's it. It's about allowing your baby to stay there as long as they need, both of you covered with a blanket if necessary. Within 40 to 120 minutes, they will look for your breast all by themselves and latch on with no trouble.

The baby will be completely content and happy, and you will be calm and celebrating the fact that your baby is there your arms.

There are many medical centers that already understand the physical, emotional, psychological and nutritional benefits of early SSC (for both baby and mother), but there are others where **only an informed and empowered mom will be strong enough to ask for skin-to-skin** (with the understanding that this only applies when both mom and baby are healthy, with no need for medical interventions after delivery).

The first hour of life is also called the **golden hour** because of how important it is from so many perspectives. Unfortunately, once it's gone you can never get it back, so, provided it is in your hands, do whatever you can to enjoy it. For your sake and your baby's.

But what if I can't do it?

We all know that births don't always go according to plan, and yes, there could be complications that prevent you from having this experience. It's not the end of the world. If, for whatever reason, you can't do it, you can always ask your partner or a family member to do skin-to-skin. Or, when you finally have your baby with you (regardless of how long you were separated), encourage yourself to make that contact that both of you will cherish so much.

Keep in mind that a lack of skin-to-skin contact at birth is one of the main reasons for difficulties in nursing. This means that, if you want to breastfeed, there is a good chance you will have trouble with latching. It's nothing that can't be solved, but this way you'll be able to handle it better and you'll be armed and ready to tackle it.

The First Three Months

Exterogestation Begins
Extero-what?!

In the moment a baby is born, we assume that there is a before and after, that they were inside the womb and now they are out, that they were a part of us before, but not anymore.

Nothing could be further from the truth.

For your baby, birth is a continuation of their development that requires basically the same conditions as when they were in your tummy. Just looking at a newborn human, it's obvious that they aren't made for this world: they can't move around, find their own food or communicate. It is clear that, without an adult to care for them, they simply would not survive.

If we compare them with other species, many other newborns come out of their mother's uterus already walking, eating and looking after themselves. **We humans are born before we're ready**. In fact, some anthropologists have presented theories that our pregnancies used to be twenty-one months, but with evolution, the human head has become bigger while women's hips have become narrower due to bipedalism (the act of walking on two legs), which essentially made nature say, "Okay, there's no way the kids are going to fit through there if we wait until the end, better make them come out sooner." In other words, all humans are born premature.

Understanding that, in effect, humans do not "finish gestation" in the uterus, we can conclude that we must continue "gestating" outside of it. This is what we call *exterogestation*.

What exterogestation implies is that we attempt to replicate life inside the womb as much as possible using these two pillars:

Contact

 **IMPORTANT**

There is no greater harm to humanity than the widespread myth of "don't hold them so much or you'll spoil them". Contact for a baby or young child is not a whim, a bad habit, or something that will prevent them from being well-adjusted... it is a BASIC NEED.

Babies are in extreme contact with us for nine months; every inch of their bodies was "touched" by ours in the form of amniotic fluid. Then, they come out before they're ready, so it's logical that that need to feel us close by would persist.

Cradling, rocking, holding them close to your chest with the sound of your heartbeat and the warmth of your skin, is part of what helps them grow up healthily.

Constant Feeding

I present to you the second greatest harm to humanity: the widespread myth that you "have to feed them every 3 hours/you have to schedule their feeds/you should make them "grin and bear it" a little longer without eating. Just like contact, food in the womb was not limited. Any time your baby felt the need, they would just "open their mouth" and eat.

That is why both breastfeeding and formula feeding should be done on demand. Babies don't have vices, they won't get spoiled, they don't ask to be fed on a whim. They ask for it out of need, and it is a need that we must fulfill.

It's normal...

I understand that, for many, this information will break deeply internalized paradigms. All our lives, we've heard that you'll spoil a baby if you hold them too much, that they need to sleep in their cribs, that they need to eat on a schedule, and reading the exact opposite might make you feel conflicted. **But nature is wise, and science has given us guidelines**: a child wanting to be held, or only sleeping on mom or dad, or asking for the breast or bottle often, or being anxious in highchairs, swings or their crib, isn't just normal—it's what allows them to develop in the best way possible.

So, I invite you to not only do away with the labels that your baby is profligate, manipulative or demanding, but also to stop fighting against nature and let yourself be guided by love and that need that you will feel yourself when your baby is always near you. It's what you both need.

Our Emotions Set the Bar

Exterogestation doesn't just have physical implications, like the need to be held or fed constantly; it is also said that there is an invisible umbilical cord, through which mother and baby are connected by their emotions.

Some authors explain that, if a baby is crying inconsolably, after ruling out possible medical explanations, the best thing is to take your eyes off the baby and turn them to the mother. Determine: How does the mom feel? Is she being supported by her partner/family? Does she feel comfortable in her new role as mother?

Usually, the "cure" to a crying baby lies in the answer to these questions. The baby, still being (virtually) part of the mother, seems to be capable of not just capturing her emotions, but manifesting them. **They say that the baby cries what the mother keeps quiet.**

> They say that it takes a village to raise a child... There is so much truth in that saying. The mother needs to be deeply and constantly supported by loved ones (partner, family, friends), because mom's emotional wellbeing translates to the overall wellbeing of the baby. So, if you are pregnant or have a young child, assemble your tribe.

Talk with your partner/family, explain that what you need is for them to let you forget about other tasks so that you can focus on your baby. Try to build a support network that takes care of you so that you can effectively and affectively take care of your child.

Breast or Bottle Feeding. What Do / Want?

The ever-present feud of breastmilk vs. formula may seem heated at times, and less intense at others, but it is definitely not going anywhere. We will always find comments and opinions from both sides arguing that their way is best.

The type of food you give your baby is one of the cornerstones of Informed Childrearing. It is one of the most critical and transcendental decisions in raising your child. Not so much because of the food per se, but because of the actions you take based on that decision. That's why you need to take time to define what you want in order to know what you will do with your baby.

When making any decision, the logical thing to do is weigh several factors. In raising a child, those could be: your needs as a mom, your child's needs, external circumstances, expert recommendations, etc.

If we go off of the needs of the baby and what the experts say (and by experts I am referring to institutions like the World Health Organization, the American Academy of Pediatrics, and the Spanish Association of Pediatrics, to name a few), the answer is very simple: **the only food is breastmilk, and it will be their main source of nutrition until their first birthday.** It is true that baby formula is a food that is considered suitable for human consumption, but breastmilk is what they should receive. Now, I'm not trying to demonize formula (it is, in fact, a life-saving food), but we should be clear that mother's milk is what we should offer them, and formula is something that seeks to replace what we should be offering. No point in fooling ourselves.

However… it is understood that the needs and preferences of the mother also need to be considered when making decisions. And this is where the real work comes in, in asking yourself: What do I want? Do I really understand all the implications of breastfeeding? Do I understand all the adverse effects of formula? What am I willing to sacrifice? (Because both require sacrifices.)

A mom who decides not to breastfeed is not "less" of a mom, nor is she a "bad" mother. But the only way she will be at peace with not breastfeeding and not feel the need to apologize to the world (and to herself) is if she has really been mindful in making that decision, if she put the factors on the scales and weighed *all* of them (even the ones she doesn't want to hear).

On the other hand, one who decides she does want to breastfeed needs to go through her own decision-making process, too. She needs to know what to expect, how it works, and what to do in the face of very probable obstacles.

This brings us to the question: what about moms who *can't* breastfeed? (I once read about a survey where 60 to 70% of the women interviewed at a medical center said that they didn't produce sufficient milk or that they were unable to nurse.) Here is another key concept: I won't say all, but 95% of women in the world have the physical capacity to breastfeed, and their babies the capacity to receive their milk, so if you are reading, you most likely do not have any physical condition that will keep you from nursing…

But (and it's a big "but"), not every woman has the emotional capacities to breastfeed. By emotional capacities, I am referring to: having enough support, being able to trust their own bodies, reconciling with the fact that their lives will not be the same, accepting that they won't be able to keep their social or work life intact, having enough inner strength to face the challenges and/or to get a second opinion (when healthcare workers give you misguided recommendations based on outdated information), having the tools to give yourself body and soul to the feeding of your child and enjoying the process. This is why breastfeeding fails. Not because of insufficient milk, or poor-quality milk, or gluttonous, demanding babies, but because *we are not emotionally prepared for what is coming.*

This is why it's so fundamental to define what you want. If you make a mindful decision that you want to breastfeed and you prepare yourself emotionally, you'll know that one of the pillars is having proper support and that the majority of stories of breastfeeding failure are not because of medical conditions which render the mother unable to feed her baby, but rather because of lack of information, insecurity, myths, old-fashioned medical professionals, lack of support, etc.

 **IMPORTANT**

Both breastfeeding and bottle feeding have their science, their challenges and their considerations. For both, you'll need to educate yourself. For both, you'll need to be at peace with the decision.

Starting to Breastfeed

While this is not a book dedicated to breastfeeding, statistically speaking, most mothers want to breastfeed, and most do for a short period of time. For this reason, I thought it was important to do a section on starting to breastfeed and what happens with it.

According to data from the Spanish Association of Pediatrics, 72.4% of mothers start to breastfeed, holding steady up to six weeks (71%) but then decreasing to 66% at three months and, by six months, only 47.9% are still breastfeeding, only to decrease tremendously to 28.5% after six months.

How is it that only one out of three or four babies manages to receive what national and world health organizations recommend, which is breastmilk as the main food until one year of age, and then continuing until at least the second birthday?

Again, because **we're not prepared**. And by preparation, I mean the intellectual/academic and emotional parts, since physically there are no objections; our bodies do everything just the way they should.

Unfortunately, the most common difficulties which lead us to stop nursing are all preventable or "treatable". The problem is that we have a healthcare system (worldwide) that isn't up-to-date or equipped to help the peripartum woman in her struggles with lactation, to the point that it's the medical professionals themselves who interfere in this delicate process, and the mothers, in general, don't have adequate support.

Something that I emphasize to mothers in my lactation course and sessions: **breastfeeding ought to be instinctive, natural, and something that happens automatically, but it isn't.**

In the past, when absolutely every woman nursed, when there was less intervention in births, when mothers' only task was to dedicate themselves to their baby, breastfeeding was instinctive. But now, with unnecessary interventions in births, with women who are expected to breastfeed, work, cook, and take care of their partners on top of being fit and dressing fashionably, we can no longer say that we have a strong enough connection with that primitive state that lactation requires.

Ironically, we have to be very informed and empowered to give ourselves permission to connect with that instinct. Without information, we will be too unsure of ourselves to go with the flow during the experience. Without information, we are doomed to letting ourselves be guided by myths, misguided remarks and outdated medical recommendations.

In addition to studying, there is another pillar of successful breastfeeding: having adequate support that allows for you to develop emotionally in this process. Starting with your family, and extending to working hand-in-hand with a specialist in this field as your guide, someone who has dedicated themselves specifically to the study of breastfeeding.

Unfortunately, many healthcare workers, in their position as experts and purveyors of knowledge, confuse mothers with nonsense; that their milk isn't satiating or they aren't producing enough, that the baby doesn't like it, or is intolerant or allergic to his mother's milk, that they should give the baby a bottle so that he sleeps more (something proven to be untrue), that the baby needs a fixed schedule for feedings, that they shouldn't let the baby "use them as a pacifier", that they shouldn't hold the baby so much, that he needs to cry it out... Basically, if I made a list of all the false claims made by many medical professionals, which only serve to disconnect us even further from our essence, it would take up this entire book.

A fundamental principle of Informed Childrea-ring is that we must have criteria to examine, but we must feed **those criteria**. So I'm going to take this opportunity to share my personal ten commandments of breastfeeding to give you someplace to start on the subject and, from there, take flight, prepare yourself and feed your criteria as much as possible:

1. **Get informed in advance** and have access to a lactation specialist who can support you if necessary.

2. **Breastfeeding shouldn't hurt** (I hope the bold font here will express the importance of this point). Cracked nipples aren't normal. If it hurts, call a specialist.

3. **Avoid using bottles or pacifiers** for at least the first month (if you need to supplement, bottles aren't necessary, but in any case, call your lactation specialist).

4. **Never use your pump** to measure your milk (that's not how it works).

5. **Understand that feeding is on demand**, without schedules or time limits (and, if you see that the "demand" is excessive, there might be a problem, and you should consult a specialist).

6. **Breastfeeding isn't linear**: it has peaks (growth spurts) where the baby will demand more, and then it will "level off". This is normal and it isn't necessary to give additional milk.

7. **Doctors and other healthcare workers**, generally speaking, **are not prepared and do not have the updated information** to help you. Be very cautious with the recommendations you receive.

8. **No breastmilk is poor quality** or "doesn't agree" with a baby. There is no such thing as breastmilk intolerance or a baby who is allergic to their mother's milk.

9. **Between 95 and 98% of women can**, physically, **breastfeed**, and for those who (physically) can't, it's because they have an underlying medical condition, diagnosed and confirmed that is interfering with their ability to nurse.

10. While almost all women are physiologically capable of breastfeeding, **most are not emotionally prepared for the challenge**.

 **IMPORTANT**

Whether you are pregnant or already have your baby, if you have trouble nursing but you want to breastfeed, seek out specialized help, educate yourself in a timely manner, and have a specialist give you the emotional tools to deal with the difficulties, and you'll see that breastfeeding without feeling stressed or overwhelmed, and having your baby grow up healthy, is possible.

Late Nights

We tend to associate motherhood with lack of sleep, and I think this is one of the few paradigms that is actually true.

Not sleeping, or rather, having your sleep constantly interrupted, is horrible. There's no way to sugarcoat it. Interrupted sleep makes us irritable and wears through our patience, both of which make raising children *very* difficult.

And this is where I present the magical solution. The technique that will make your baby sleep through the night... Oh, did you think I was serious? 😌 If I had the answer, I'd sell it for millions (and people would pay), so I wouldn't share it in this book 😈.

Okay, all joking aside, there is a lot to be said on the topic of babies' sleep. There are several schools of thought and theories that give guidelines on how a baby's sleep should be. The goal of this chapter is to explain that there are several ways to interpret infant sleep and for you to use your Informed Childrearing to decide what you want for your family.

Although in this first stage (from 0 to 3 months) there will be sleepless nights, nighttime feedings and a few other difficulties, sleep is not *that* difficult to manage. The reason is that, because of sleep's evolutionary characteristics, at this stage babies fall asleep fairly easily. They will fall asleep at the breast, rocking them gently, or they will even be awake and then, in the blink of an eye, fall asleep all by themselves. And, when they are asleep, they tend to sleep very, very deeply.

However, this won't always be the case, and later on you will run into "sleep issues", and, as a result, you will be desperately looking for solutions.

After a lot of reading and research, I could summarize by saying that there are basically two philosophies related to sleep. **One is based on the idea that babies' sleep is not only "modifiable" by adults, but that it is our responsibility to make sure the child sleeps x hours a day on a specific schedule**. In addition, it includes a series of recommended strategies for parents to get their children to sleep. The methods are varied, such as ignoring the baby's cries so that they know it's bedtime, doing what is called "controlled crying" in which parents leave the room for a certain amount of time, or another that consists of going into the room but not picking the baby up to soothe them, among others. And, the common suggestion of proponents of this style is that, as parents, we should habituate our children to sleeping on their own, to not needing to be fed or rocked in order to fall asleep.

The other philosophy is the complete opposite. In this case, it is based on the theory that **babies' sleep is an evolutionary process comparable to the ability to walk**. That, just as we can't force a child to walk at six months old, we can't force a baby to not wake up in the middle of the night. It explains that nighttime awakening is not just normal, but necessary, and seeking to eliminate it with any technique is incoherent with human nature. Likewise, it is categorically opposed to ignoring a baby's crying. The reason for this is that studies have shown that crying causes excessive cortisol production (the stress hormone), which has harmful emotional, psychological, mental and even physical effects.

Do they really "learn" to sleep by crying?

After several days of "training", we have seen or heard from parents who state that their babies do not, in fact, wake up in the night anymore. But what's really going on here? When babies are alone, their first thought is that mom and dad have vanished, and consequently, "I'm at the mercy of predators" (for babies there is no difference between being alone in their crib or alone in the jungle; it is the same sense of danger). That is why they cry, to ensure that their caretakers are, well, taking care of them. When we don't respond to their crying, the baby will feel more and more stress, and their crying will intensify proportionally. Some "techniques" say that you can go into the room but not pick up the baby, just talk to them... the thing is, in these cases, when the baby is crying so hard and has such a high level of stress, a mother can be standing right next to the baby without them even realizing she's there. In these cases, physical contact is essential to "pull" the baby out of that "high alert" state that they are in.

If we continue to ignore their crying, we could say that the baby's brain concludes, "Okay, no one is coming to help me, so I'm alone. If I want to survive, I'd better be quiet so that the predators don't find me." On a physical level, this means that, in the face of excessive stress hormone that "drugs" the baby (some even vomit when they are in this state), the body secretes calming hormones to counter that stress, putting the baby to sleep thanks to a combination of exhaustion and hormones released as a defense mechanism.

After several days of this hormonal dynamic, the child will stop waking up, but not because they have learned to sleep, rather, **because they have learned that they are alone**.

If you are a mom who used these methods and this explanation makes you feel guilt or remorse, I understand. I did it with my first child, and it was very hard for me to process this information and make peace with the decision I made back them. **My goal is not to upset you, judge you or make you judge yourself.** It's to offer information, even when it's something you don't want to hear (or read, in this case) and encourage you to change things going forward ☻. Sometimes, we have the information beforehand, and other times we find it along the way; it will always be beneficial, it will always be worth taking it into account. That's what Informed Childrearing is about.

So, what can we do?

The solution for interrupted sleep is simple. If your doctor told you that for the next year, you had to take a pill every night at 2 a.m. and 5 a.m., what would you do? You wouldn't say that the medicine is "supposed" to be in the dining room and the water in the kitchen, making yourself get up twice in the middle of the night to get both things. You'd make sure everything was handy, the medicine and the water, on your nightstand, right? Do the same thing with your baby. If you know that you'll have to tend to them in the middle of the night, make your life easier and keep them nearby! The solution is to have the baby sleep very close to their parents, satisfying a human child's innate need for company and making nighttime awakenings less annoying for the parents. It could be in a crib in mom and dad's room or even in the same bed (what we call *co-sleeping*).

Knowing that there are two schools of thought (and that they are so different from each other) helps you to be properly informed and decide which is more compatible with your lifestyle.

I'm taking the liberty of addressing the subject as a person who is not only a mother, but also someone who works with mothers and answers their concerns every day. I, personally, lean towards the second philosophy.

Considering that **crying is a baby's only means of communication**, it seems cruel to me to ignore it, even for limited times. Furthermore, **babies have no notion of time and space**. They are incapable of comprehending the concept of mom being someplace else and that she will come back soon. If a baby does not sense that they are near their caregiver, **they feel completely helpless**, and it would be a shame for our babies to have this feeling of abandonment and **perceive the world as a hostile place**, so soon after they arrive in this world. Besides, if I saw my partner, my mother, or my neighbor crying, I would go up to them and try to help... why wouldn't I extend the same courtesy to my children?

On the other hand, the notion that the number of hours a child sleeps depends on the parent **can absolutely destroy our perception of how we are doing as parents**. The less your child sleeps, the more frustrated you become, with feelings of failure and guilt. This emotional cocktail, on top of the lack of sleep, is enough to make you *lose your mind*. Too many mothers, under the premise that they "should" make sure that their children sleep *x* number of hours, feel like bad mothers, incompetent mothers, which then fills them with even more insecurity and mistrust in themselves.

Isn't there some intermediate option that doesn't involve leaving the baby to cry, but also doesn't involve putting him in bed with me? Yes, maybe, but I doubt you'll find it in any book; this is something that each family must figure out by observing their own family dynamic and their baby's patterns and trying alternatives to put them to bed in a way that (ideally) is agreeable for both the parents and the child.

In conclusion, a whole other book could be written about sleep. But for starters, know that there are options, and try to research them to determine what works better for you. For this sort of thing, it's best to use your Informed Childrearing, investigate and inquire, and discover your own path before repeating what others have done.

You're probably wondering: is there any difference in sleep between babies who are breastfed and babies who are bottle fed? No, they both wake up the same amount. Sleep is not conditioned by the type of food and not all babies necessarily wake up because they are hungry. So the practice of giving them a bottle—or even worse, baby cereal—so that they sleep more is not only harmful, but also ineffective.

The Pacifier Dilemma

To use or not to use a pacifier, that is the question.

If it's bad for breastfeeding or for their teeth, if it protects against sudden infant death syndrome (SIDS), if you don't give it to them they'll use you as a pacifier and then you'll really be sorry...

Pacifiers are one of the main "focuses" of opinions about mothers. The fact of the matter is, like everything in motherhood, there are good and not so good things about pacifiers. Ultimately, whether or not to use it is a completely personal decision, and I hope that this chapter will help you make that decision.

First of all, I'd like to get one thing straight: **the problem isn't so much the pacifier itself, but rather its excessive use**. As such, using it once in a while is not the same as the baby using it practically all day long.

Let's start by clarifying that pacifiers are not necessary for a baby's development. You won't regret not using it, nor will you make your life worse if your baby doesn't use it. Don't worry; babies will always have demands, and really, when they cry, what's best for them is that their caregivers figure out what they need, not "shut them up" with a pacifier.

Babies may need many things, but sucking is an indulgence and a big distraction. That's why pacifiers make them stop crying so quickly and easily, even if we might not have solved the real "problem". It's possible that they need food or direct contact with mom's body heat, that they are bothered by something around them, but they get a pacifier, and it distracts them. I think it's important to clarify that *I do not mean to say* that mothers who use them are not paying attention to their babies' needs; all I want to do is put into context how we, sometimes inadvertently, abuse this resource and make it our automatic and almost immediate response to any demand from our baby.

This is the reason why I'm not crazy **about pacifiers. Not so much because of their implications in breastfeeding or how they affect the teeth and speech, but because of the emotional component that we attribute to them. Here's my one hundred percent personal opinion: I like my children to find consolation in things that are more "real", like a hug, a word of encouragement, contact with other people and the empathy of others, rather than in a pacifier. I expect that, as they learn to look to others for support, it will be a way to teach them how to support others in the future and be empathetic.**

As It Relates to Breastfeeding

Pacifiers have two basic problems: 1) they can interfere with the baby's sucking pattern so that they do not know how to latch onto the breast later, and 2) in many cases, they are used to "stretch" feedings. These two situations are classics in cases of unsuccessful breastfeeding: it happens that the baby refuses the mother's breast, that it hurts them to nurse or they don't gain weight and, in the end, the cause of it all was an excessive use of pacifiers. The literature recommends avoiding pacifiers until "breastfeeding is established". But when is that? It's relative. Each mom and baby, each experience and each story is its own world. That's why there's no "real" answer to when you can use a pacifier. It's left up to your judgment, although most people agree that they should be avoided during the first month of life.

He Won't Use Me as a Pacifier?

This is a fear that has been instilled in mothers... But I ask you, what came first? The boob or the binky? Babies are wired to have a sucking reflex, and that reflex has, in principle, one purpose: so that babies can feed themselves. So, if they need to suck, they will ask for food or, perhaps, suck on their hands. But where we often get confused is the following: yes, the baby has a need to suck, but not to suck on "whatever"; they need to suck on a breast. Satisfying their need to suckle with a pacifier turns that reflex (which was initially a survival measure) into a habit established for our convenience.

So, no, they're not using you as a pacifier, they're using you as a mom. It's not about just suckling, it's about your presence, your scent, the sounds made by your body. It's about you being their universe, and they will always need you, with or without a pacifier.

Pacifiers and Teeth

It is true that excessive use of pacifiers can alter the anatomy and development of the oral cavity in babies; however, this occurs when it is used for more than three years. So, if you decide to use it, try to make sure it isn't used beyond that age; before then, there is no reason to be afraid of it.

What Is It Good For?

If you decide to use it, it can be particularly useful if you are traveling by car and your little one won't calm down, if you want them to relax and sleep or on other occasions where you don't want to offer them a breast. Some evidence suggests (but does not explain why) that there could be a relationship between use of a pacifier and lower incidence of SIDS.

So, What Do You Recommend?

I recommend that you take the time to decide what you want to do. That you use your Informed Childrearing and that you do not use a pacifier out of fear, because of other people's remarks or just because that is just what people do. And if you do use it, keep in mind that pacifiers have nutritional and emotional considerations too, so they shouldn't be abused. Not abusing means:

» Not extending feedings with a pacifier.

» Not replacing nighttime feedings with it (at least not for the 12 months that breastmilk is your baby's main food).

» Not leaving it attached to their clothing all day (this provides very easy and constant access).

» Not using it immediately every time your child cries; instead, offer other resources to calm them down.

» Trying not to let them spend hours with the pacifier in their mouth, playing with the pacifier, going out for a walk with the pacifier, everything with the pacifier (this can even interfere with speech development).

» Planning on weaning **progressively** off of it from two years of age so that, ideally, they stop using it by age three.

Pacifiers are neither a panacea nor a basic necessity for you to not wear yourself out meeting the demands of your baby; likewise, it isn't a demon that dooms breastfeeding to failure, wreaks havoc on teeth or emotionally impairs children. It simply has its good parts and not so good parts. *It has its considerations* and I invite you to keep them in mind when determining if you want to use it or not.

Three to six months

A decline in breastfeeding

After three months is when breastfeeding starts to dwindle among mothers. One reason is a return to work (which we will talk about later on), and another is the "three-month crisis", which I would like to prepare you for.

This crisis is the combination of many natural and normal phenomena of breastfeeding, but if you aren't familiar with them, you can easily fall into despair. I'll explain the factors one by one.

"My breasts are soft, I must have dried up"

Prior to the three-month mark, our bodies are determining what our babies need (because every mother produces the amount of milk her baby needs). Moms produce milk constantly, our breasts feel heavy, and sometimes they leak. Well, as it happens, after approximately three months, the dynamic changes: the body now knows what the baby's needs are, and instead of producing milk constantly, the "factory" is activated when the baby latches onto the breast. In other words, milk starts being produced then and there. The brain detects the stimulus from the suckling and says to the glands, "All right, get to work!"

This means that, in this stage, most women stop feeling that their breasts are full, instead noticing that they are soft all the time and no longer leaking. Many think that these manifestations mean that they no longer have milk, but that's not true. What's happened is that their bodies have self-regulated, and, from now on, they will activate when the baby needs it, without "disturbing us" between feedings.

"My Baby Is Fighting the Breast"

As I said, now, milk is produced when the baby starts nursing. And so, the process goes like this: the baby latches onto the breast, the brain detects the "there's a hungry baby here" signal and puts the glands to work. The thing is, the mammary glands take a minute or two to produce milk.

For a baby who is used to the milk coming out immediately, the fact that there is now a two-minute delay is not funny at all. That's why they fight the breast. Not because your "production is down", but because they are anxious because their food isn't coming at the rate they want; but the milk **always** comes. It's no big deal and nothing that time won't solve. It's just a matter of them adapting to the new dynamic.

However, **another reason that they can start to fight is the use of bottles**. After a few months, a baby who used to have no trouble breastfeeding or bottle feeding (even with breastmilk) can go on what is called a "nursing strike" and prefer a bottle over the breast. In these cases, depending on the degree of refusal, it can be managed in different ways, so the best option is to contact a lactation consultant.

"He's Done in Five Minutes, He Can't Possibly Be Full"

After breastfeeding a newborn who can nurse for half an hour (which is normal), it can be shocking and disconcerting when, all of a sudden, the baby gets full in five minutes and sometimes as little as three.

At three months, your body isn't the only thing changing—your baby is, too. By now, they're experts at suckling and don't need as much time to extract the milk they need, and they can see better now (before this, their vision is blurry and colorless), so everything catches their eye. They get distracted, they want to explore, so they eat fast so that they can move on to something more interesting.

"His Weight Has Plateaued"

The characteristics typical of this stage, such as distractions, quick feedings, and the time it takes for the milk to come out, can in some cases have repercussions on the baby's weight. And there's nothing that mothers fear more than weigh-ins at the pediatrician's office, am I right?

While a baby's growth is an extremely important indicator of his nutrition and development, it is equally important to point out that, in this stage, it's normal for there not to be as much of an increase in weight, and that doesn't necessarily mean that you need to supplement with extra milk. A "not great" weigh-in should not condemn breastfeeding as long as the other health indicators are maintained: consistent pee, yellow poop, happy baby. It's fine to just pay attention at the next checkup or, when in doubt, consult a lactation specialist.

"He Used to Sleep Several Hours at a Time and Now He Wakes Up Every Hour and a Half; He Must Be Hungry"

When a baby "regresses" in his sleep, it's common for the mother to think he hasn't had enough milk. In the next chapter, I'll address this concern.

Sleep Regression?

In the first three months, I mentioned that in most but not all cases, babies tend to fall asleep easily and stay deeply asleep without much effort on our part.

There is also this notion that, as the child gets older, he'll sleep more. No, mommies, it usually gets *worse* 😄. One of the questions I get most often about sleep is that babies who are three, four or five months old go from sleeping six to eight hours at a time at night to waking up "like a newborn or worse", that is, every hour and a half or two hours.

What happened? Is my baby regressing? Have I run out of milk? No, your production isn't low and there is no regression happening; it's more like an evolution, just one that isn't a lot of fun for us.

The best explanation I know of about how infant sleep works comes from child psychologist and psychopediatrician Rosa Jove. Very briefly, I will tell you how sleep works: human sleep cycles are made up of five stages: we go from wakefulness to stage 1 of transitioning to sleep, stage 2 of light sleep, stages 3 and 4 of deep sleep, up to the fifth stage, which is REM sleep (this is when we dream). Newborns only have two of these stages (light sleep and REM), which is why they tend to fall asleep quickly and sleep very deeply. However, at four months (and until six months), all of the sleep stages are incorporated. So, what's the problem? Well, it's difficult for babies to weave one stage into another, and they wake up every time they come out of a stage, leading to very frequent and bothersome (bothersome for the parents, the babies don't even notice) nighttime awakenings.

Knowing that this can happen helps us to be prepared. Part of implementing Informed Childrearing is knowing the natural processes in children and not having unrealistic expectations. It's very common for parents, ignorant of how infant sleep evolves in this phase, to think that they have done something wrong or that their baby has some sort of problem when they start to wake up more often.

The way to manage this phase is, firstly, with lots of patience; it is usually a temporary phase, and it is very important that you not try to interfere in the process or take measures that can lead to sleep aversion later on, or distrust the human body by giving them artificial milk, foods or baby cereal.

Give Food Now or at Six Months, That's the Dilemma

Starting to give foods to your baby is a whole new stage, and an exciting one for parents. But, like everything in motherhood, we find ourselves with a decision that stirs controversy: *when to start.*

On this matter, you'll find two types of pediatricians: those who, at four to five months, tell you, "You can start introducing foods now," and accompany this statement with a sheet explaining the types of foods, amounts and instructions to prepare baby food purees, and those who say no foods until they are at least six months old. Which ones are right?

In healthcare, recommendations are made based on scientific and statistical studies: data are collected from millions of people and the results are analyzed to reach a consensus on different health issues. Because of this, when health organizations like the WHO or the Spanish Association of Pediatrics recommend something, they are backing that up with enough statistical data to make it a trustworthy suggestion.

With this in mind, the WHO says, and I quote, "WHO recommends mothers worldwide to exclusively breastfeed infants for the child's first six months to achieve optimal growth, development and health. Thereafter, they should be given nutritious complementary foods and continue breastfeeding up to the age of two years or beyond."

By exclusively breastfeed, they mean that we should not incorporate anything other than breastmilk (including foods, obviously) until six months of age. And the same applies to bottle fed babies: only milk until six months. "But I gave my kid soups at four months and he's very healthy and happy," is a typical response from some mothers. I want to clarify, giving foods before six months is not a matter of "life and death"; babies *are* capable of taking and managing foods from four months old. But just because they are *capable*, just because it is possible to give them foods, doesn't mean that it is what's best for them, not by a long shot.

Some reasons why you should wait (Source – Spanish Association of Pediatrics):

» There is no food with more complete nutrition than breastmilk (or, failing that, formula); giving foods too early fills the baby's stomach with less nourishing contents.

» There is a greater risk of gastrointestinal infections.

» They do not have the necessary enzymes for good digestion (at four months, pancreatic amylase is low or practically nonexistent).

» The kidneys are not ready to manage the solutes that come from food.

» There is an increased risk of allergies.

> When making any decision, you can weigh the pros and cons. If you do this with foods, you will see that there are many possible complications and that it really doesn't offer any benefit if they start to eat sooner.

Even so, it is common to hear people give these reasons for starting to feed with other foods. I'll list and explain them, in case you have the same questions.

» **The baby hasn't gained enough weight.** When a baby isn't growing properly, the "treatment" isn't to give him food, but rather to identify the cause with the help of a lactation consultant. Giving other foods will have the opposite effect, and he could lose even more weight because baby food tends to be less calorie-dense and less nutritious than breastmilk or formula.

» **The baby looked like he wanted to try the food.** Babies are attracted to everything we do and will always try to imitate it. It's logical and natural for them to show interest, but that doesn't mean that they are ready.

» **The baby is sleeping very little.** Sleep, as we've seen, is the source of a lot of grief for families. Also, there is a belief that, if they eat more, they will sleep better. However, there is no evidence to support this (and no, what your cousin told you doesn't count as evidence 😬). *Sleep is completely unrelated to the amount of food they eat.*

» **He needs to get used to it so he won't be a picky eater in the future**. It's a popular belief, but there is no study showing a relationship between when you start to introduce foods and their "taste" for foods in the future.

» **It's to prevent allergies**. There is some confusion on the subject of allergies. Years ago, it was concluded (after many studies) that it was best to incorporate potentially allergenic foods *early* to prevent allergies. Now, of course, *early* means as soon as possible, but after six months, when the body is immunologically prepared for it. Some interpret this as the earlier the better, but that is not the case.

So, why did my pediatrician tell me to start introducing foods? Honestly, I don't know. Considering how concrete the evidence is, and how clear the recommendations of WHO, AAP and other institutions are, I do not understand why they would tell you any different. I mean, starting with foods before that isn't life or death, but when you weigh everything, it brings more risks than benefits, so what's the point?

This is the importance of Informed Childrearing, to use your judgment, to be discerning, and, when in doubt, you can always seek a second opinion from another pediatrician.

Back to Work

"Our children need us at home." I understand that this statement will cause feelings of conflict and chagrin for many readers. But I'm coming from a basic premise of raising children: acceptance is better than denial.

The more we as parents can accept reality (even when we do not like it), the more we will be able to be proactive, look for solutions or find ways to live with those realities and with as few obstacles as possible.

There are two realities that relate to returning to work:

» **Our children need us at home.** Babies and small children are creatures who are dependent on their caregivers and especially on their mothers. Women, after giving birth, are not moms with a baby but rather a "mom-baby" dyad that is joined by an emotional and spiritual thread. That connection is precisely what has allowed humanity to survive, giving mothers the primordial task of looking out for the health of their offspring. Our children need our milk, our warmth, our voice, our scent. They need it to feel safe and contained and for optimal emotional and mental development.

» **Demanding that a woman leave her baby to go back to work is a sign that our society has its priorities all wrong.** Society insists that each individual must fulfill a "productive function" within it, and dedicating oneself to raising and molding future world leaders is not considered productive. How can that be? The lack of recognition of childrearing together with the modern trend of household expenses being covered by both parents (when the father is present) makes women feel a financial, social and personal need to return to work. And this is how the mothers of the world overload themselves with maintaining our work life and having the energy and emotional availability to raise children (in addition to looking pretty, eating healthy and going out with friends).

After going back to work, dealing with dirty diapers, crying fits and late nights *is a gargantuan task*. But since most women do it, we assume that it's "normal". But it's not—they, and we, are demanding too much of us.

There's a reason why all, or almost all, mothers have a major emotional conflict when they have to return to work. We are being asked to leave our primal function, the one dictated by our genetic code, to do something else.

I Don't Want to Leave My Baby, But I Need the Money

Let's say you had a friend who's been working for some years at a company. He doesn't love his job, but he doesn't hate it either and it pays the bills, which is what really matters. He goes in every day, does what he is supposed to do (and not poorly), but, in his head, he is waiting to clock out and dedicate himself to what really makes his heart full: painting. And even when he dedicates some time to it after work and on weekends, he isn't satisfied. He always feels that he'd like to dedicate more time to painting, which is what really makes him happy.

What do you think is best for your friend? Should he leave that mediocre job forever and use his enthusiasm to explore his passion or find a way to combine his work with what he loves?

If we talk about "anyone else" in terms of working at what they love, it is completely acceptable to motivate that person to explore the possibility of leaving a conventional job, to tell them to get creative with other ways to earn money and/or do away with some material conveniences so that they can spend more time doing what fulfills them... so, why don't we look at raising kids in the same way?

I'm giving all this introduction because I know that, if the first thing you read was: be creative, find an unconventional way to earn money, and set aside some comforts to reduce expenses so that you can dedicate yourself to your children, you would close the book and call me crazy. But if deep down you want to dedicate more time to your kids, don't ignore that need, don't repress it saying things like, "If I don't work, how will we eat?" or "You've got to make a living."

The goal of this chapter is not to encourage you to abandon your career and then "see what happens"; it's just a nudge for you to assess what fulfills you, what you want to do and what makes you happy. If what you want is to spend more time with your children, don't wait until they're grown up and you regret not having been with them enough... Check out your options, step out of your comfort zone, make changes and never stop looking for your way to be happy (which can be applied to childrearing or to anything else). At least give yourself permission to explore the possibilities: it could be starting a small business, offering some service from home, working part-time—there are alternatives, you just have to look for them.

Motherhood, far from being a disadvantage, can be an opportunity to reinvent yourself, always in search of your wellbeing.

I Don't Want to Leave My Baby, But I Really Like My Job and I Want to Go Back

It might be that the need to return to work isn't purely financial, but also social, one of personal fulfillment or enjoyment. Wanting to go back to work doesn't make you a bad mother or inferior to one who stays at home.

Enjoying raising your children implies that you are satisfied. If what satisfies you is your career, then that is exactly what your kids need. The good thing about your motives not being solely financial is that you don't have that pressure, and you can always divide your time the way you see fit.

What matters isn't that you meet a quota of time with your children; again, what matters is that you are happy and look out for your *wellbeing*.

If You Spend a Lot of Time Out of the House

If, by choice or by necessity, you spend much of your day away from home, you should remember the fact that our children need us close by. So, if you can't spend a lot of time with your children, make sure you do spend high-quality time with them.

It's very easy for a mother who is at home all day not to have quality time with her baby. Basically, you need to prioritize those moments of connection and harmony so that they don't fall by the wayside, regardless of whether you are a full-time mom or you work outside the home all day.

As I said before, working so many hours only to later deal with the ups and downs of raising children is a gargantuan task. But, both you and your baby need lots of time for love, connection, play, or just to be together and spend time with each other. If you are out of the house many hours a day, make sure that when you come home, you are as mentally and emotionally present for your baby as you can be. This means setting your phone down and making household chores secondary. If you have a lot to do, try to involve your baby, letting them join you while you cook (you can tell them about your day or describe what you are doing as you do it), or you can use a baby carrier to get the most out of every minute and keep them very close to you. Try to be present (really present) in routine tasks like baths, dinner and bedtime. In fact, many families practice co-sleeping (mom and baby sleeping in the same bed) as a way to "recover" some lost time, as well as dealing with the child's usual awakenings so that they can get a little more rest at night.

Motherhood has multiple dimensions; it can be lived very differently by each mother, and working or not working really doesn't define what type of mother you are.

Besides, life is too short to spend most of your time doing something that isn't 100% fulfilling for you. A mother who works and is sad and not content with her reality is unlikely to have the necessary mental peace to manage her children at home. Or, conversely, if you are a full-time mother and you miss that feeling from working, and this makes you unhappy with yourself, then it will be just as difficult to find quality time and authentic enjoyment in what you are doing.

It doesn't matter which is your reality, as long as you are at peace with it and you are prioritizing your own wellbeing so that you can look after your children's wellbeing.

Are Breastfeeding and Work Compatible?

One of the reasons why many mothers give up on their desire to breastfeed is because they have to return to work. Nursing implies being present, which is why it is thought that breastfeeding is incompatible with a woman rejoining the workforce, but no, they are not incompatible.

I won't deny that it is a tough logistical challenge, but with determination, support and consistency, it can be done. Let's be clear that it is much easier for caretakers and for the mother herself to offer formula, which is why **continuing with breastfeeding begins with the mother's decision to do so**. The more sure you are of what you want, the better you will be able to find the tools to achieve it.

Like everything in motherhood, and it is one of the pillars of Informed Childrearing, once you know what you want to do, the second step is to *prepare* yourself. In many cases, mothers make the mistake of pumping milk and saving it without any sort of guide. And so, there are those who produce lots of milk, who achieve their goal because their bodies are in harmony with what they want and their life doesn't making things too complicated. But there are other mothers (I'd say the majority) who, in their attempt to extract milk for their babies, find that they don't get as much as they expected, assume that they aren't producing enough, and give up.

Lactation consultants aren't just there when you have a problem nursing, but we are also there for you to guide you in this sort of process, so that you can achieve your breastfeeding goals even if you go back to work.

Continuing to breastfeed while returning to work is possible if the mother prepares a homemade milk bank (pumping milk and storing it to be given to the baby by the caregiver). This undoubtedly comes with many challenges, and I'll tell you some of them so that you can be a little more "prepared" for what it entails:

» **Not enough milk is coming out to store.** One of the major downfalls of breastfeeding is the breast pump. When a mother applies the device and sees that she isn't getting as much as she expected, her confidence is destroyed and she falls into a spiral of doubts about her body and her production. So I want to clarify: a baby can be perfectly fed from a mother whose production is perfect and the pump can still wind up almost empty. There is no comparison between a baby's suckling and the mechanical movement of the pump. Having set that straight, I also know that not being able to pump enough milk *is a problem for working mothers.* The solution for this isn't a pill or concoction—there are no potions that increase production—but in doing *effective* extraction. Properly stimulating the hormones (relaxed state, massaging the breast and nipple, etc.) and having the correct pace for pumping. Ideally, you would even pump one breast while nursing with the other, and yes, I know you're thinking that that's impossible, but it can be done, and it is, in fact, the best way to extract milk.

» **A decrease in production at some point**. If a mother is separated from her baby and doesn't nurse over the course of the workday, it's a fact that her production will decline. The body interprets the lack of suction as the baby not needing as much milk anymore and says, "Why work more? Lower production!" The way to avoid this is by pumping in the workplace. This keeps prolactin (the hormone that "makes" the milk) levels high and always producing.

» **The baby doesn't want to nurse**. I wish it weren't so... but daily use of bottles can, sooner or later, after days or months, confuse the baby so that he refuses his mother's breast. In fact, no baby has ever "weaned himself at ten months", as you sometimes hear; this is usually a symptom of confusion from the use of bottles. This is why lactation consultants advise against them. Did you know that there are other ways besides bottles to offer milk? Depending on who is taking care of your baby, you'll be looking at people who are more or less willing to try alternatives to offer breastmilk. There are little cups (specially designed to feed babies, or you can use any small cup), feeding with a syringe or bottles that have a small spoon or training cup instead of a nipple. If you will be away from your baby for a long period of time, it would be best for you to explore these options and mention them to your child's caregiver. Let me be clear: bottles are the easiest 😋. All of these alternatives are a little more complicated, but nothing that can't be mastered with a little practice and technique.

Are there bottles that won't confuse the baby and won't cause them to refuse to nurse? Marketing says yes, but the evidence doesn't confirm this. In other words, in the absence of specific studies, I don't trust any bottle, no matter what the brand may advertise. What does exist is a technique to offer a bottle in a way that is more "amicable" to breastfeeding. It's called the Kassing method (I won't go into it more here, but I mention it so that you can look it up yourself).

» **The baby won't take the bottle**. If a mother has breastfed the whole time, it could be that the baby doesn't like to eat from a bottle. For these children, look for alternatives! Your baby is very smart and doesn't want to be confused.

💡 TIP

In addition to these challenges, there is the overwhelm that mothers feel while pumping, maintaining a milk bank with a sufficient amount of milk and handling it properly so that the milk doesn't go bad. If you need to go back to work and are distressed by the subject of a milk bank, get help! That's what we're here for.

To the Floor!

Motor development is one the aspects that evolves the most in a baby from 0 to 12 months. They go from hardly moving at all to, in many cases, walking, or at least crawling around. Many, many changes take place from birth and a large number of mothers have questions about what they should do so that their babies develop properly. Do we need to stimulate our babies for them to achieve these things? You might think that you need to attend special early enrichment classes or do exercises at home...

 EYE!

Movement in babies is not something that we need to "teach", but rather something that we need to "allow".

By this, I mean that there is nothing specific you have to do as parents (unless you suspect your baby has some developmental delay), no exercise or activity; just **give them freedom to move about the house.**

This is why, around three months, we take it to the floor! It's the perfect place for little ones to get excited about moving around. Starting with the ability to raise their head and neck when facedown, then rolling over, and finally moving around and exploring their surroundings.

If you really want to be proactive in your baby's motor development, make sure you have a physical space that allows him free movement and exploration. Some of the characteristics this space should have that I can share with you are the following (applicable from three months onward):

» Again, it should be on the **floor**. Think about it: they can't fall from there, so it's much safer to place your baby there than on a bed or sofa.

» Look for a **soft but firm surface**. You can use your favorite rug (preferably not a shag rug for hygiene reasons). There are many on the market, both fabric and foam.

» **Make sure he has things of different heights around.** Something as simple as a sofa, coffee table, and a little chair is perfect so that they can later support themselves and learn to stand up.

» **Avoid excessive toys.** If you want to motivate your child to move around, having lots of things around them can be counterproductive. It will be very hard for them to choose an object and move towards it. So, clear everything away and show them something that will get their attention (although nothing is as effective as you yourself ☺).

» **Dress them appropriately**. As long as the temperature permits, the less clothing, the better! When it's cold out, it's worth turning up the heat (even if it's just for a little while) so that you can put your baby in comfortable, lightweight clothing that allows them to move around.

On the other hand, you can't just create the right physical space, but it is also important to offer an *emotional space* that aids in the process. Keep in mind that the development of motor milestones is a great challenge for babies, one that can be frustrating and requires a lot of courage. That's why having a good physical space has no more weight than offering that emotional support. How?

» Always maintain a positive attitude; try not to transmit your fears to them. Set aside the "be careful," "you're going to fall," "don't break that," "you're too little for that," etc. and strive to give them encouragement and always motivate them to overcome those obstacles.

» Join them in the process, play an active part. This means being physically and emotionally available, motivating them and making the experience a fun moment for everyone. It's possible for babies to get frustrated in the process, so your closeness will make the difference in whether or not they are excited to keep trying. Also, remember that labels never help, so be careful not to fall into the trap of making comments that they are fearful/cowardly/weak. Every child will go at a different pace, and we must respect that.

With regard to pacing: motor milestones have approximate ages when they should be reached. As it is not my field, I don't want to delve specifically into that subject, but it's enough to compare your baby to *several* (I repeat, several) babies of the same age. If you see a marked difference, you can always ask your pediatrician or physiotherapist.

When a baby has a motor delay, it is very common that, beyond the baby "having a problem", we have made a mistake as parents, in not letting them "doing their thing" and move around. We live in a society filled with baby strollers, swings, seesaws, highchairs and playpens that limit their play space; while convenient, excessive use can have repercussions on their development.

As a final reflection, it can also happen that, when a baby doesn't hit a certain milestone or does so more slowly (but within the normal range), we feel we might be doing something wrong and may even hear ignorant comments on the matter that make us feel worse. So, bear in mind that whether they reach a milestone sooner or later does not determine your capacity as a parent. And, when in doubt, you can always consult a specialist.

Should I Clean His Mouth?

Many parents have very little idea about when or how to start oral hygiene in children. But this habit is fundamental in the prevention of one of the most common diseases in the world: tooth decay. The number of children (and adults) who have tooth decay is alarming, and it is only by establishing healthy habits that we can ensure our children don't get it. For those who think that cavities are an inevitable part of childhood, I want to clarify that they are not. Cavities are 100% preventable.

Tooth decay depends on many factors, but hygiene is one of the most important. When we begin is key in instilling this habit successfully.

> 💡 **TIP**
>
> The ideal time to start is at four months, when their immune system is a little more developed. In starting hygiene at this age, the goal isn't so much to remove bacteria from the oral cavity, but rather to get the baby used to you poking around in their mouth (which is very important to ensure their cooperation in the future).

For your baby's oral hygiene, you should take advantage of a calm and quiet moment; bath time is perfect. Wash your hands thoroughly and wrap your finger in sterile gauze moistened with (warm) boiled water. Then, gently massage their gums, tongue and the roof of their mouth, and enjoy the moment.

I'll bet you didn't know oral hygiene started so early, did you?

Six Months

Time to Eat!
How Do I Know If My Baby Is Ready?

Being able to introduce foods is an exciting moment, isn't it? If you happened to find an up-to-date, pro-breast-feeding pediatrician or if you have done the research yourself, you'll know that *starting from* six months, you can start to give them foods. But did you know that age is not the only factor to consider?

Being six months old is the first requirement, but there are other signs that will help you to know that your baby is, in fact, ready to eat. Here they are:

» **They've lost the extrusion or tongue-thrust reflex.** This reflex is what makes your baby use their little tongue to push out anything that isn't liquid. It's one of the body's defense mechanisms (the body is very smart) to protect the baby from eating anything other than milk, because they aren't ready for it yet. This is why, sometimes, when starting foods too early, parents will suffer and complain that their babies "spit" out all their porridge and push the spoon out with their tongue. It's their way of telling us, "No, Mommy, I can't eat this yet."

» **They take things in their hands and put them in their mouths**. This is another developmental sign that shows they can eat.

» **They can sit up in their highchair (with support)**. I invite you to try eating a puree or drinking a glass of water lying down. It is extremely uncomfortable. Even if we are relaxing on the beach or in bed, we always sit up to eat or drink anything. The same goes for our babies. Giving food to a baby who can't hold his head up means he must be fed lying down. This is not just uncomfortable, but it also makes him more prone to choking. So, for safety reasons, it's better if he can sit up with back support.

» **They are interested in the foods**. While there are babies who seem desperate to eat, there are others who will put absolutely everything in their mouths, unless it's food. Interest is another way of telling us whether they are ready or not.

Some babies do not show these signs at six months and need a little more time. Remember that milk, whether breastmilk or formula, is the main food source for babies until 12 months; this removes some of the pressure to make them eat "ASAP" because we know that they are well-nourished by the milk they are eating, and we can give them a margin of a few weeks. In any case, I go into this information in more detail in my nutrition course, and you can also consult with your pediatrician.

Doing Things Differently

Like everything in childrearing, nutrition is not exempt from social paradigms that have been instilled in us for generations. But let's take a look at the results of these "rules" about how we should eat that have been practically ingrained in us by our parents and grandparents. The most recent study on the child population (Aladino, 2015) determined that 43% of Spanish children are overweight/obese, and that we are the country with the most obese children in Europe. Similarly, some studies have concluded that, on average, Spaniards consume four times more sugar than the recommended daily amount from the WHO.

It's Time for Us to Do Things Differently

Doing things differently means changing our way of looking at infancy and nutrition. There is a general belief that candy is an inherent part of a happy childhood, or that cookies are a valid way of showing affection, or that "this is how we ate back in my day, and look at me!" which gives us permission to repeat the same patterns.

There are studies concluding that it seems that sugar and other unhealthy foods have an addictive component because of their chemical effects on the brain. But did you know there is also a psychological or emotional addiction? This relationship that we adults encourage in a child is what creates, little by little, an adult who eats for emotional reasons, who "rewards" themselves with unhealthy foods, and, in general, develops an unhealthy relationship with food that leads to the statistics mentioned above.

Doing things differently means separating happiness, success and personal realization from sweets the same way they were synonymous for us. For example, things like, "If you're good, I'll give you a chocolate", "Clean your plate or no dessert", "Today's a special day! Let's get ice cream", or the fact that gifts for any occasion involve candy, all send a message to children that sweets are how we show love, appreciation or some kind of success.

Doing things differently means understanding that being a kid doesn't have to be synonymous with eating junk. There are millions of things that make us think that a child without candy "has no childhood or won't be as happy", and much of this is because of constant advertising and what we saw in our own childhoods. We associate sweets with love because that's what we were taught to do.

The next time you are thinking about showing your children affection with something sweet, I invite you to pause for a moment and consider showing affection with affection: with quality time, with play, doing an activity that the child enjoys, with kisses, with walks, not with candy, and tell me how it goes!

Doing things differently also means actually *doing things differently*. I grew up drinking chocolate milk and juice boxes and eating sweets, and I turned out "fine" (in quotes because "fine" is relative). I personally might not be overweight or obese, but it is a fact that millions of children and adults are. What is more, statistically, there is a 50% chance that you, dear reader, are overweight to some degree. So, are you sure you want to leave your child's health up to chance? I'd rather be proactive, understand the fundamentals of a healthy relationship with food, and not repeat the same patterns just because "that's how my mom did it", and I encourage you to do the same ☺.

Clarification: my goal is not to eradicate candy from the world, and I'm not saying that we should completely give up eating sweets. All this means is not "adding fuel to the fire", not making a habit out of it or exalting something that is proven to be harmful. Not repeating patterns out of inertia, separating affection from unhealthy food (because there's no reason for the two to be related), and questioning what "everyone else does" to forge our own path without prejudices. Informed Childrearing before all else.

Doing things differently starts with the beginning of complementary foods. Had you stopped to think that, at six months old, your baby is starting a practice that will stay with them for the rest of their life? The way in which you offer foods (especially the emotional context) will have a major impact on their relationship with food.

So yes, I invite you to use your Informed Childrearing, to expand your knowledge about food for babies and small children, to not give food out of inertia, buying them whatever you were bought or whatever the big brands are selling. I invite you to do things differently so that we can change the statistics.

Breastmilk/Formula and Foods. How Do They Mix?

When starting to give food, one of the questions that arises is, "But when do I give him milk? Which one is more important?"

Going back to my friend, the Spanish Association of Pediatrics, in several of their publications, they explain that milk should continue to be the baby's main food until twelve months; in other words, you should continue to nurse on demand *at least* four or five times a day.
What does that mean?

» You shouldn't replace breast or bottle feedings with foods.

» If your baby doesn't want to eat, you can rest assured that the milk is keeping them nourished.

» Breastmilk continues to be nutritional and necessary. It doesn't "turn into water" after six months, or ever.

» If your baby is hungry, you should offer what you know will satisfy their hunger: milk.

Between six and twelve months, **feeding takes on a connotation that is more educational than nutritional**. We need to give babies time and space to get used to foods, to enjoy eating them and to appreciate their natural textures and flavors. Making sure the baby enjoys it is the priority, and knowing that the milk is nourishing them removes some of the pressure with regard to the amount of food that you think they should be eating.

The idea is for foods to *progressively* gain prominence from six to twelve months; in other words, you've got half a year to get there. In the meantime, milk is fundamental, it is their main food and so it must come first.

Solids at Six Months!
What Madness Is This!

Imagine a baby born centuries ago when there were no blenders, food processers or anything like that—how do you think they ate? Easy! As they were gaining their motor skills, they ate the same way as their parents! There wasn't much to think about.

However, we evolved, studied and created protocols, and this is where we begin the chronicles of complementary feeding and the different ways of starting it. At some point in history, the nutritional recommendation was to start offering food to babies starting at four months, or even three. This made it imperative to use food that was possible for such a tiny, tiny baby to process, thus giving birth to the concept of baby purees and baby food. However, based on evidence, that recommendation was changed to say that babies should start to eat at six months. At this age, babies already have a motor capacity that is very different from what they had at three or four months. Now, they can hold things in their hands, put them in their mouths, sit upright with support—*it's completely different.*

If you set aside the social paradigms about baby nutrition and carefully observe your own baby, you will see that, in fact, they can eat solid foods and they can do it all by themselves.

This is the basis of the feeding method known as *Baby Led Weaning* (or BLW for short). It involves offering babies, starting at six months, foods in their natural state or the same way we would normally eat them, completely skipping the "baby food phase".

This method goes beyond offering solids. The basic premise is making the baby the protagonist of their feeding experience. In other words, we give them the opportunity to experiment with food, to decide what (of the things on the table) they want most, and, most of all, *how much of it to eat.* This is in contrast to baby food where the adult is in control of everything: what the baby eats (mixing whatever the pediatrician has indicated together so you can't tell anything apart); when they should eat (usually setting a schedule at our discretion); and *how much* they should eat (preparing *x* amount of food and making sure they eat all of it, using strategies like shaking a rattle, the airplane or choo-choo-train trick, or even worse, relying on a tablet or phone to help us accomplish our goal).

 EYE!

Deciding to use BLW involves something difficult: giving up control. It means allowing your baby to experiment with food, which translates to very messy hands, hair, face, highchair and floor, and letting them eat as much as their body says they need (which may seem like little to us, but they know what they need better than we do).

Relinquishing control is so hard for us that it leads many people to immediately reject this method (especially grandparents). We think that "he'll never eat enough that way", "he'll spend his whole life eating with his hands", "he's going to be malnourished", and we think that it's madness to give solids at six months.

And, another reason baby led weaning is so shocking and crazy sounding is **fear that the baby will choke**. Fear of choking is no small thing, and I will never tell you to "relax" or say "there's no reason to worry". Obviously, there are certain common-sense rules to ensure the baby can eat without being in any danger. For example:

» **They must really be ready**. They need to show the signs explained in the chapter "How do I know if he can eat yet?"

» **The right texture**. The food must have a firm texture so that the baby can pick it up, but also soft enough to process it without teeth. A good test is that you can smash the food easily between your fingers.

» **The way you offer the food**. It should be cut in such a way that your baby, with their clumsy little hands, can pick the food up and chew at it. For example, thick sticks of vegetables or fruit, or circular shapes like a hamburger or pancake that they can hold in both hands. Until nine or ten months, avoid any presentation that can be eaten in one bite, like banana slices or cubed watermelon, which are difficult for them to manage.

» **Completely avoid round foods**. Such as cherries, cherry tomatoes, grapes, olives, and hard foods like nuts or uncooked apple. You can also completely rule out hotdogs, which are terrible nutritionally anyway.

» **Finally and most importantly for your baby's safety: know what you're doing**. Wanting to try BLW is, to me, a good decision considering its benefits. But you must *never* do it without having first prepared yourself. This means having attended a course, having support from an expert in the subject or having read sufficiently. In other words, having a deep understanding of the method, knowing what's normal and what's not, in-depth research on the subject of choking, and feeling very, very empowered to offer solids without fear or stress. It's essential, both to reap the benefits of this method and for your baby's safety, that you feel comfortable.

Forbidden in Feeding

I don't like to talk about "forbidden things" in general, but I'll use it now as a way to convey the importance of what I will explain below. Starting to give a baby food, like everything in motherhood, is a responsibility. So, taking on that responsibility obviously implies that there are things you need to avoid for your child's wellbeing, both in terms of nutrition and physical health as well as emotional, as it relates to their relationship with food. That is why I decided to write this chapter and call it "forbidden in feeding"; those things are:

» **Forcing them to eat.** Never, ever, no matter how desperate you feel, whether because of pressure from your mother in law or because your baby is underweight, never force them to eat. This is the first big forbidden thing. Forcing them to eat is one of the most common ways we disrespect our children and their bodies. And we do it in ways that seem subtle, like, "make sure you clean your plate", "you can't do such and such until you eat", "mommy gets sad when you don't eat", etc. One of the consequences of saying these things, or other similar actions, is that we teach our children to systematically ignore their hunger signals, to associate a clean plate with their appreciation of you, putting them at risk of becoming an adult who has a hard time knowing when or how to stop eating. It's important to be aware of what you are saying because *everything* has a deeper message. Our children's healthy relationship with food begins with us. Never forget that.

» **Distracting them to get them to eat**. This strategy is kissing cousins with forcing. It might seem harmless, or even nice, but its function is the same: for the child to eat what we want, when we want. The most used tool for this is a tablet or phone with cartoons and colors that distract the child until they stop paying attention to what their body is saying or what they want. One of the major consequences of distraction is similar to its kissing cousin: we teach them to systematically ignore the signals of fullness that their body gives them, creating a child who later won't know when they've had enough. Again, it doesn't matter how desperate you are or what the circumstances are, distracting, or more accurately, "disconnecting" kids with a tablet is not the solution; it's a band-aid that will later lead to other potentially worse problems.

» **Stressing out over food**. Usually, we perceive food as purely nutritional, but it's not; it has many other dimensions, a background of social and emotional wellbeing. What feeling do you want to transmit at mealtime? Stress, overwhelm, fighting, an unpleasant experience, or an enjoyable, satisfying moment shared with family? Recognizing what we feel and why we feel that way allows us to ask for help or make changes to manage whatever is causing us stress. The same goes for food. If it's something that is overwhelming you, there are many of us in the world of motherhood + nutrition and we can help you.

» **Taking away milk/formula so that they "eat more"**. We have already clarified that a child who asks for milk over food isn't doing so on a whim, but out of necessity. Until twelve months, it is their main food, and after that, it is still important, even if it isn't the main one anymore. In any case, a baby who "doesn't eat" isn't "not eating" because of milk. You would have to look into many other things, and, in short, taking away breastmilk or formula will not be the answer.

» **Giving sugar before one year (or even two)**. This is where many will say, "What? Why so long? This author's totally overreacting!" I'll explain: our babies have a "virgin" palate; they haven't been tainted by the excessively sweet and salty flavors in modern foods. They have the opportunity to come into the world of food with an appreciation of their natural flavors. Why would we ruin it with sweetened yogurt if they have the ability to love plain yogurt? I know why... Because we, the parents, are *so* used to sweet that unsweetened yogurt seems awful, and it doesn't seem "fair" to give it to our babies. But you and I are the ones with the "damaged" palates; theirs are perfect and it's not worth it for us to change that on a whim. It isn't easy to make sure a child doesn't eat sugar in the first years of their life, but it's not because of the child themselves, but rather the pressure from family members and friends and that social conditioning that stalks us: "Oh, a kid who doesn't eat sweets, how sad", "You're taking away his childhood", "We all grew up eating candy", and so on, as you well know by now.

» **Offering highly processed foods in their diet**. Highly processed foods are made in factories where they add excessive sugar, salt, refined oils and additives. I would go so far as to say that half of your supermarket is replete with highly processed foods, and, even worse, highly processed baby foods. If you decide to feed purees to your baby, try to avoid the ones from the supermarket, or at least read the ingredients carefully to ensure there is no salt, sugar, refined oils or additives, something that will be very difficult to find. There are many "baby products" that are not at all advisable: the famous baby cereals, herbal teas, cookies, and the list goes on. These foods tend to be very cheap, convenient and what we would call "palatable", meaning they are designed for us to like them through certain additives whose very purpose is to make it hard for us to stop eating them. The later and the less we expose our children to these "temptations", the better.

» To wrap up, there are **some foods that,** according to various organizations, **should be avoided** until one year or later, and I've shared them here for your reference.

— **Cow's milk**: Until twelve months, due to the high level of protein it contains (unnecessary for babies) and the fact that it reduces iron absorption, which is very important at this age. Also, it often triggers reactions in babies.

— **Honey**: Until two years. Honey can contain spores of an organism called *Clostridium botulinum*, which is the agent that causes botulism, a potentially fatal disease.

— **Chard and spinach**: Until twelve months. Here, many will say, "But how can that be, if it's so healthy?" The Spanish Agency for Food Safety and Nutrition explains that chard and spinach contain high levels of nitrates. Babies are not able to metabolize these nitrates, which means they can reach toxic levels, causing methemoglobinemia, a condition that affects the transport of oxygen in the blood and is responsible for the so-called blue baby syndrome. If you do offer these foods, they should make up no more than 20% of the meal.

— **Fruit juice**: You might think I mean packaged juices, but no, this also includes fresh squeezed, all-natural juice. The American Academy of Pediatrics changed their recommendations on juices, explaining that, while fruit is healthy, fruit juice lacks fiber and protein, and its high sugar content contributes to excessive consumption of calories and unhealthy weight gain, plus increasing the risk of cavities. So, no, mommies, no juice until twelve months.

— **Whole nuts**: Due to the risk of choking, these should be avoided until the child is two to four years old (depending on which book you read).

However, you can offer nuts in the form of nut butters, as long as they are natural and without sugar or other additives. Regarding allergies, new evidence suggests that a delay in offering foods, rather than protecting children from allergies, makes them more prone to them. For this reason, generally speaking, potentially allergenic foods can be offered in a way that is suitable for babies starting from six months. In any case, it is best to talk to your pediatrician about this subject in particular.

Babies Who Don't Eat Enough

One of the biggest stressors at mealtime is the amount of food that our children consume. If you are lucky enough to have a "good eater", you might feel fulfilled and satisfied, but if it seems like your baby doesn't want to eat anything, you're probably having a nervous breakdown, right?

When it comes to feeding babies, I have two basic premises:

» It is impossible to know how hungry another person is. We could make deductions based on what we know about that person or when their last meal was, but knowing how hungry they are? Impossible.

» Babies are instinctive and know what they need better than we do. Adults are the ones who are conditioned with food; we're the ones who go crazy during the holidays because we "have permission" or we'll just go on a diet before summer. We reward ourselves with a cake and refuse our vegetables. Babies don't. For them, everything is new, everything is equally interesting, and no, they haven't been conditioned yet.

If a child doesn't eat much at any given moment, it's for a simple reason: they don't need the food right now.

Remember that before they are one year old, babies' main food, what will most nourish them, is milk (breastmilk or formula), and in this stage, the purpose of feeding is educational, exploratory, one of familiarization and enjoyment.

Is Your Baby Really Not Eating, Or Do You Just Think He's Not Eating?

Look carefully at what this question implies: when we say that our babies "aren't eating", there is a lot of our own perception involved.

I read a study once where they gave a questionnaire to parents about their children's eating habits. Almost 80% said that their children ate too little, and, in turn, almost the same percentage were offering more food than was appropriate for the age of the children in question. In other words, we tend to have unrealistic expectations about what our babies should eat, and that's why we think that they eat too little or don't eat at all when that's not really the case.

So, how much should a baby eat? There is no general answer. Every baby is completely different and has different conditions that will make them more or less prone to eating large quantities of food.

I know it's hard for us to relinquish control and trust our babies. We live in a society where we are expected to have everything under control, and it helps us feel sure of ourselves to measure every ounce of food that our children consume. But **there are things that you can't control, and your baby's hunger is one of them**. The way to remove some of the pressure regarding the amount of food is by observing your baby. You think they aren't eating enough, fine, but are they growing? Are they reaching maturity milestones for their age? Has your pediatrician said there is no cause for alarm? Then stop worrying.

 **IMPORTANT**

The only thing you need to worry about is that you are offering high-quality, natural foods, and that you are meeting your baby's essential nutritional needs with foods. This way, however little he eats, it will at least be very nutritious.

I won't go into detail about the nutrients that a six-month-old baby needs, but there are many resources at your disposal: firstly, your pediatrician, and if you have further questions, you can get information from a child nutritionist and consult books, courses, etc.

Okay, now we understand that when a baby "doesn't eat enough" it is often because the parents have unrealistic expectations, or they don't need a lot of food so long as they are developing correctly... but what do you do when a baby really does have a growth problem or some sort of deficiency?

If we're talking about a baby who is less than twelve months old, the first step would be to look into how the birth went (to see if any circumstances could have an impact on their development), and then you would review **their milk consumption** (breastmilk or formula). Only after ensuring that they are consuming enough milk would you look at the subject of foods, and in that case, the right person is a professional child nutritionist. The nutritionist can create a meal plan and give parents guidelines so that, however little the baby may be eating, it will be covering their nutritional needs. We should always seek ways for them to be nourished, without ever falling into strategies that do not respect their bodies, such as forcing or distracting them, or giving them medications to "whet their appetite".

Don't Put That in Your Mouth!

I'll bet that this is the number one phrase most uttered by parents of six-month-old babies, even more than "I love you". Have you noticed?

Let's start at the beginning. Why do babies put everything in their mouths? This is what is called the mouthing stage, in which babies feel a compelling need to suck on everything they see. There are many reasons why babies put things in their mouths:

» **For pleasure**. Sucking is a means of survival for babies, and this reflex is the reason they are able to feed themselves, but it also represents consolation and satisfaction. For babies, being able to suck on different things is an enriching and, as I said, pleasurable activity.

» **To explore**. Babies' mouths are the most sensitive part of their bodies, even more than their hands. Because of this, for them to "get to know" an object, it isn't enough to look at it or touch it; they need to put it in their mouths. This is how they begin to understand the world and the objects that comprise it. They discover that there are different textures and sensations, temperatures and sizes, gathering important information about what is around them.

» **To enhance cognitive development**. Closely related to the ability to explore is your baby's ability to learn. The more things they "suck", the more they will learn.

» **As part of language development**. Many experts also assert that the opportunity to explore with their mouths helps significantly with language development.

Telling a baby not to put something in their mouth 1) doesn't work, because they aren't able to codify this instruction and maintain it over time, and 2) is a way of cutting off the baby's basic need for development, as fundamental as eating or sleeping.

When we repeat, excessively, that common phrase, "Don't put that in your mouth," we are telling our babies not to explore, not to learn. Furthermore, we are prohibiting them from doing something that they innately *need* to do, which can have an emotional impact as well. Imagine if you needed to scratch an itch and you weren't allowed to; I'd become desperate, wouldn't you?

You might understand the reasons for and benefits of the mouthing stage perfectly, but when your baby puts something in his mouth, the first thing that pops into your head is "no!" It happens to me. We're so used to hearing it, and our parents told us the same thing, so we are programmed to repeat this pattern. So, the next time your baby puts something in his mouth that he "shouldn't", and you hear that you are going to blurt out that phrase, try this: "Matthew! Don't... (pause to reconfigure your autopilot...) Don't put *that* in your mouth, try this instead," and offer him something different 😎.

How to Let Your Baby Explore Without Dying of Anxiety

I understand that the matter of safety is vital and that many of you are concerned about your babies' wellbeing with the things they put in their mouths, so I have some tips for you.

» **Anticipation**. Before letting your baby "loose" anywhere, check out what things she has nearby, because what is nearby will, inevitably, go in her mouth. If you see something dangerous, remove it.

» **Prepare the environment**. With a baby who can move around and wants to touch/suck on everything, it's best to take away anything fragile or dangerous from the start.

» **There are more harmless things than you expect.** You might think that the only safe thing for a baby to suck on are his toys, but the truth is that many things in your home are perfectly "suckable" and shouldn't be cause for concern. If your baby grabs a piece of clothing, a kitchen utensil (that's not sharp), his big brother's ruler or things like that, you can let him explore. Just be sure that the object isn't sharp, isn't small (and can't be broken into small pieces) and isn't electric.

» **Not everything will be perfectly clean**. It's important to make an effort to keep items at a certain level of hygiene, but you can't expect everything to be clean. Sometimes, you just have to take a deep breath and let it happen. If you go to the beach or a park, for example, accept the fact that she will inevitably eat a bit of sand or grass, respectively.

» **Distraction**. If your little one picks up something that he shouldn't, before telling him to stop what he's doing, offer him something better. At this age, babies are extremely easy to distract with something else.

» **Exploit their need to put things in their mouths**. There is an activity called *patuque*, from a Venezuelan word whose meaning approximately translates to getting messy or smearing. It consists of placing a tablecloth on the floor and setting your baby there (wearing only a diaper, if the temperature permits) with some foods that she has tried before. Then, you let her pick up the foods, squash them, rub them on her body, put them in her mouth and spit them out. It's a very positive sensory activity where they can satisfy their need to explore in a safe environment.

Teething

Another milestone at this age is the emergence of the first teeth!

Tooth eruption begins at approximately six months. By approximately, I mean that six months is an average; it's normal for them to come out slightly sooner or later. Some moms worry when they don't see any teeth poking out at six months... if this is you, I have good news: it's better for them to come out later! Several studies have shown that there is a relationship between the amount of time that the teeth are in the mouth and the risk of cavities, and they conclude that the later the teeth erupt, the lower the risk of cavities ☺.

On the other hand, there are many myths surrounding this event: that it causes diarrhea, fever, irritability, excess saliva, keeps them from sleeping, etc. In fact, many mothers medicate their babies when they are in the midst of teething.

What is really happening during teething?

It is not known for certain whether tooth eruption actually bothers babies, but it is true that most mothers get overwhelmed and agonize over the subject, attributing "symptoms" to teething that really have nothing to do with it.

» **Excessive saliva**. This has more to do with the baby's stage of development than the emergence of teeth. It just so happens that they drool a lot at six months because they are unable to swallow their saliva all the time. You'll see that there are babies who have a lot of saliva but don't get their first tooth until months later.

» **Diarrhea or fever**. Evidence has debunked the myth that teething causes any sort of illness. What can happen is the following: at six months, for developmental reasons, babies tend to put everything in their mouths, as we said before. So, this near constant contact with the ground and all of its bacteria can make your child ill. Whether it's to explore or because their gums really are bothering them, they will put dirty things in their mouths and that can make them sick, which is normal and something you can't control.

» **Trouble sleeping**. Again, we do not know for certain whether teething bothers babies to the point that they can't sleep. But we do know that, at six months, the sleep pattern is irregular; they can change a lot and wake up constantly during the night. Because of this, it's hard to blame teething for this situation.

The reason why I'm explaining all this is to **prevent the routine, unnecessary medication of babies** as much as possible. We tend to blame teething for all the "peculiarities" of this stage when it's possible that the changes in health or mood have more to do with the baby's age than with tooth eruption. Consider that tooth eruption will continue until three years of age, and I have seen very few mothers agonizing over teething in a two-year-old. It is unlikely that teeth have *so many* implications that only manifest at six months and not afterwards.

What can you do, then? If your baby seems irritable and you want to do what you can to help them, a good idea is to make little breastmilk or formula popsicles. It's a safe way to soothe any discomfort they may have, and it's fun for your baby!

Get the Toothbrush and the Dentist!

Once the first tooth comes out, there are two important changes: 1) you need to start using a toothbrush and toothpaste, and 2) you need to visit the dentist for the first time.

People tend to disregard toothbrushing in babies, but keep in mind that, where there are teeth, there can be cavities. So, whether they have one tooth or ten, you need to take care of them to keep them from getting damaged. The right way to do this is with a small toothbrush and toothpaste with fluoride (yes, you read that right), a concentration of 1000 ppm or 0.24% sodium fluoride or 0.76% sodium monofluorophosphate (jot these numbers down). Most children's toothpastes have less fluoride than they should, so I recommend that you flip the product over and check the concentration instead of going by the suggested ages advertised by the manufacturer.

1000 ppm of fluoride is a lot of fluoride; you need to be aware of that and use the toothpaste responsibly, keeping it out of reach of children and using the correct dosage to avoid excessive ingestion.

— For babies from their first tooth to two years: an amount equivalent to half a grain of uncooked rice.

— For children two to four years old: an amount equivalent to one grain of cooked rice.

— From four years on (if they know how to spit by now): a pea-sized amount.

As additional information, it's better to "smush" the toothpaste into the bristles and not wet the brush before putting it in their mouth in order to reduce the risk of fluoride ingestion. In any case, part of the reason it's so important to go to a pediatric dentist when the first tooth erupts is so that he or she can give you hygiene guidelines tailored to your baby.

Eight to Twelve Months

This is one of the most common complaints among mothers of babies around eight months old. Many claim that it's as if their baby has been "replaced with another". Before, he was so calm, and now they can't even go to the bathroom without him crying.

What's Going on With Babies at This Age?

Remember that exterogestation thing? Well, it is at approximately this age that it starts to break. Before eight months, your baby genuinely believes that the two of you are the same person. The connection is so deep that they feel as though they were still in the womb. Around eight months, as your child matures and starts to understand the world, they are struck by a terrifying reality: "My mom is one person and I'm another, which means we can be separated."

When babies reach this inevitable conclusion, they enter a sort of crisis, in which they are afraid to lose sight of their mom because they are scared that she won't come back. This is what we call **separation anxiety**. If you add this to the fact that they have no comprehension of time and space, you can understand the despair they must feel if we walk away, even if it's just for a minute. For babies at this age, if they don't see their mom, she has ceased to exist; in other words, they are incapable of understanding that mom exists in another space. Similarly, they have no notion of time; for a baby, leaving her for a minute is exactly as terrifying as leaving her for an hour, and the more time goes by, the more stress hormones are produced, which have an effect on her development. In fact, from the first instant, they are already on high alert.

Other things that happen in this period: they want to feed like crazy (it's their way of saying, "if mom wants to leave, I'll cling to her chest), they sleep worse because they wake up to make sure that mom is nearby, and they are reluctant to be held by other people.

All of this is normal. It can't be fixed with "techniques" and it doesn't mean the child is spoiled. The best way to get through this phase is by giving them a strong feeling of security and stability, reassuring them that mommy is there. If you are going to leave them in somebody else's care, say goodbye to them, even if they cry, because it's their way of knowing that, when mom leaves, they'll know about it first, and you won't just "disappear" without warning.

This can be a tough stage, but it will pass, I promise. Stay sane and don't listen to anyone who tells you to ignore your baby. Ignoring them is leaving them immersed in fear and anxiety.

Child-Ready Environment

Don't think for a second that babies can understand rules—it's better to have the environment ready for them.

How many times has it happened to you, or you have seen it happen to other mothers, that you repeat an instruction one and a half billion times, and the baby doesn't listen.

» "Don't touch the socket"

» "Don't throw things"

» "Don't get the wall dirty"

» "That's not for eating"

» "Stop sucking on the furniture"

» "Don't touch that, it's fragile"

» "Don't climb up there, you'll fall"

    ... and so on, ad infinitum.

Let's get one thing clear: until approximately age three, children are completely incapable of understanding a rule, let alone maintaining it over time. And prior to two years, I would say don't even bother with explaining that an electrical outlet can give them a "booboo". Before two years, the area where you should invest most of your energy is in getting the environment ready and childproofed. A childproof environment allows you to:

» Give your child the appropriate space to meet a basic need: exploration. And as we know by now, exploration means touching and sucking on everything, climbing and experimenting with throwing things.

» Avoid constantly fighting and spending all day telling them what not to do.

» Protect your baby from getting hurt.

» Protect your valuables from being "manhandled" by your child.

I know that grandparents will go off saying that they always kept their living room as it is and their children "never touched anything". Okay, 1) I don't believe that at all, and 2) if that was the case, at what cost? Fighting, yelling, frustration, spanking? It isn't worth it.

We all want a house decorated like a magazine, but the sooner we realize that this is incompatible with an exploring baby, the better. This keeps you from having a bad time of it. Informed Childrearing, among other things, invites us to inform ourselves about our children's capacities at every stage. Understanding that they do not, in fact, have the capacity to comprehend and maintain a rule is the way for us to have realistic expectations. Don't feel like a "bad mother", that you're "doing it wrong" or "your child is spoiled" just because they go and touch a lamp despite the fact that you've told them twenty times not to. Information sets realistic expectations, and realistic expectations reduce frustration and allow us to enjoy raising our children more, don't you think?

So, what is a child-ready environment? It is a space designed with your little one in mind, in terms of both safety and exploration and learning. Its goal is for your home to be dedicated to their development without damage to them or your belongings. Some suggestions for preparing your environment:

» **Take away everything you don't want them to touch and put it out of their reach**. Simple. Cleaning products, the TV remote, your phone, the car keys, glass vases, the sculpture you inherited from your grandmother. If you don't want it damaged or broken, get it out of the way.

» **If you can't take it away, create a barrier**. If there's a low hutch with china in it that you can't move, or your baby loves to go into the bathroom, make sure you put up safety gates so that they can't access or open these things.

» **Protect electrical outlets**. Don't even bother explaining that they shouldn't touch sockets. Cover them safely and save yourself time and energy.

» **Prepare "creative" corners**. In different parts of the house, have a corner with a toy or item designed for your little one. For example, a chalkboard with magnetic shapes (appropriately sized) for them to explore, an area with a few sensory bottles or bags (if you don't know what these are, you can find this and how to make them online), a safe mirror at their height (Montessori mirror), anything that can stay in its place and entertain your baby with something interesting and safe to explore as they make their way throughout the house.

» **Have a toy area with just a few things, not too many and preferably toys with no lights or batteries**. Toys with lights don't usually invite much interaction. For your baby, something like a rattle, some blocks, or anything else that allows them to experiment will be much more enriching: How do I make it make noise? What happens when I throw it? What are these different textures? Etc.

» **Use safe home décor**. Having babies doesn't mean you need to have a barren house. You can always turn things around. If you have a low table that you want to decorate, you can always look for safe objects. For example: plastic picture frames (difficult to break), removing the glass. Obviously, the photo will not survive the tiny hands of an exploring baby, but you can always change it. You can use plastic vases or metal figurines that can be knocked around, use wooden boxes with "treasure" inside. Boxes are pretty and offer your baby a distraction and stress-free way to explore. You just have to get creative.

» **In the kitchen, prepare drawers that are suitable for babies**. You can fill them with kitchen utensils like whisks, spatulas, ladles, and other things they can touch (and suck on) with no problem. You can have dish towels, plastic or metal cups and bowls, pots. The kitchen is one of the most frequented rooms by family members and it can be the most enriching if you organize it with them in mind.

Baby's Sleep

Usually in these months, almost a year after the baby was born, mothers are **fed up** with their children waking them up at night. Especially if they had unrealistic expectations on the subject, like trying to get the baby to sleep twelve hours at a time at two months old in their room or having the baby in another room, which makes a restful night even harder. In the same vein, you will notice, or already have, that your baby's sleep gets *worse* over time.

In the beginning, we are all resigned to the fact that a newborn baby will wake up every night to eat, but we don't have other factors that also interfere with babies' sleep, some of which are:

» The change in sleep patterns characteristic of the baby's neurological development, which we have already discussed.

» The acquisition of motor milestones that get him "excited" and, in some cases, keep him from sleeping.

» Teething.

» Runny noses or illness.

» Some change in his life, like mom going back to work, a move, whatever the case may be.

» Having had a boring day.

» Having had a very stimulating day.

» If they need to increase your milk production, they will also wake up more at night.

» Separation anxiety.

» Feeling cold.

» Feeling hot.

» Having an itch on their big toe...

In short, any excuse is a good one for your baby to wake up more or continue to wake up in the middle of the night.

On this point, you will have tried everything you've read or been recommended: setting a nighttime routine, giving them a massage, feeding them a lot during the day (so they don't ask for it at night), scheduling feedings (I don't know why), doing activities that tire them out but don't "overstimulate" them, give them pumped breastmilk so that they "eat better and last longer", or, failing that, baby formula. You may have also tried to console the baby without feeding or tried to get them to sleep without nursing. Some, perhaps, have even resorted (successfully or unsuccessfully) to less respectful strategies, like adding cereal to their bottle or letting them cry it out.

Not only do I understand you, I share your pain because I went through it and used all the same "strategies", in my case, without success. *The point is, we're tired.* And because I know that you are or will be tired, I also know that this is the stage where we fall into a sort of desperation. I wish there was a "remedy" for nighttime awakenings, I wish that babies didn't feel the need for contact or re-assurance during the night and would let us sleep... but that's not the way it is.

The goal of this chapter is to remind you and reinforce that what you are going through is, indeed, normal. It is very hard, but it's part of the experience of being a mo-ther. Your baby isn't "spoiled", and you haven't "raised him wrong"; it's just that the rhythms of a maturing baby don't allow them to sleep as long as we want them to. By the way, for those of you who have a good sleeper, I recommend that you don't talk about it much if you don't want to be the object of envy 😬.

What alternatives exist to keep us from faltering in the task of childrearing and dealing with nighttime awake-nings? The most practical option is to keep your baby nearby. This way, you can: 1) soothe them quickly so that they don't go into heavy crying, which will be harder to stop and making it more difficult for them to get back to sleep; 2) tend to your baby without having to wake up completely, which will help you fall back asleep faster later; 3) sometimes, your baby, after merely seeing you and feeling you close, will go to sleep again without you even realizing it.

I know there are many social customs with regard to babies being in our bedrooms or our beds, but it is a practical way to tend to your baby and not be dead tired all day long. If this isn't something that you're comfortable with, you can choose the sleeping arrangements that seem best to you, understanding that your baby is going to need you just as much at night as they do during the day. We are still moms when night falls, and we still have a responsibility to console them, even if the sun is down. Find the way that gets you through this stage with the best attitude possible, and remember that **this too shall pass**. To ensure your mental health in the face of comments and recommendations from others, I'd like to give you my top ten myths about sleep 💚:

1. "Give him a little formula and see how he sleeps." Giving artificial milk doesn't make them sleep more; sleep is not regulated by their digestive system but by their nervous system.

2. "Pump your milk and give it to her separately to make sure she gets full. She'll do the same with a bottle of pumped milk." There's nothing wrong with offering pumped breastmilk, but it's extra work for mothers to extract it and it won't make any difference.

3. "He's *x* months old already, he should be sleeping longer." According to several studies, a child's sleep *begins* to resemble that of an adult at age three (yes, so don't hold your breath). It's normal for your baby to wake up (often) until that age.

4. "She's probably hungry, you must not be producing enough." Umm, no, that's got nothing to do with it.

5. "If you put him in your bed, you'll never get him out of there." Can you imagine your sixteen-year-old kid sleeping in your bed with you? It's not going to happen, even if you wanted it to. When they reach an age where they want to have more independence, and as long as you treat the matter of sleep with respect, I assure you that your baby will sleep in their crib.

6. "If you bring them into the bedroom, your marriage is over." Intimacy is not created in bed, it is just one of the many places where it manifests. Intimacy is created in good conversation, a solid relationship, feeling supported... If a marriage ends, it won't be because the baby slept in their parents' bed, but for much deeper reasons.

7. "You should take away her nighttime feedings." Many people, both healthcare workers and others, are adamant about this for reasons that are completely irrelevant. The point is, there is no evidence-based reason that says a mother should stop nursing at night.

8. "Give him water at night so he won't want to wake up anymore." Until twelve months, babies need milk; it is their main food. Giving them water would affect your baby's consumption of nutrients. If they wake up in the night, want to feed, and eat, it's because they need it.

9. "If you let them cry, in three days they'll sleep through the night." We have already touched on the subject of crying, stress, and its implications. Letting them cry is not, and will never be, the solution.

10. "My baby was already sleeping all night at two months old." The king of myths is thinking that all babies are the same. There may be some babies who do sleep more, but they are not the majority and you shouldn't assume that your baby ought to do the same.

Twelve Months

I'm all grown up, well, maybe not really...

Your baby is one year old!

So many things have happened, so many changes. It's like, as soon as you get start to get used to something, bam! Something new shows up. But you did it.

I wanted to leave you this bonus chapter because, with baby's first birthday, there will also come many new expectations from the world. At twelve months, your baby is grown, but not *that* grown. In case you reach this point and you have any questions, I've left the most common ones below for you to review as needed:

» It's normal for them to still wake up in the night.

» It's normal for them to want to nurse often (they will still need to for a while longer and, if you want to keep breastfeeding, it's normal for the demand to be high).

» It's normal for them to change their way of eating and start to eat less. This has to do with their calorie needs: after one year, a baby grows at a slower pace, and therefore doesn't need as much food.

» If they drink formula, at this age you can start offering whole dairy products instead of artificial milk, and if they are breastfed, you can offer them too, although they aren't necessary.

» Remember that they are still not capable of understanding and maintaining a rule, so you can save yourself your "no's" and your lectures. You can explain it to them, but with no expectations that you won't have to repeat things again.

» Their need to explore will grow, and you will see the benefits of your creativity in making your home "child-ready". It's normal for you to need to make some new changes at home.

» It's normal for them to start showing signs of temper tantrums.

» It's normal for you to have questions. Questions are there so that we can improve.

Epilogue

Nope, it doesn't stop

In conclusion, in each stage, there will be many expectations and things people say that your baby "should be doing or should have stopped doing by now". As you have seen, **Informed Childrearing is a process that never stops, but is with us every step of the way, in every challenge, in every moment of doubt. It gives us the chance to take our insecurities and transform them into learning and a way to grow personally and in our role as mothers**.

I hope this journey you have joined me on has given you a generalized and slightly different perspective on motherhood, babies, sleep, nursing and nutrition. I hope it encourages you, as I said, to keep investigating and educating yourself so that your Informed Childrearing grows in tandem with your baby. And better still, as you grow and empower yourself, I hope you feel comfortable enough to share your experience with Informed Childrearing with other mothers in the form of accurate and timely information. Together, we can be a source of wisdom that touches and improves the lives of many moms who desperately need it.

I am eternally thankful that you have opened the doors and let me into your motherhood and trusted me to share my view of childrearing with you. With all my heart, I hope that this book helps you to better understand your baby, that it gives you guidelines to empower you in the different aspects we mentioned, and that, ultimately, you develop all of your tools and get maximum enjoyment out of raising your children. I know we have all been told that being a mother is hard and not always enjoyable, but I truly believe that things can be different with women who are sure of themselves, satisfied, armed with their own criteria in the face of others' opinions, empowered, and able to seek help and know where to find it. I hope that this message has reached you in every single line I have written. Because being happy moms is the only way we can have happy babies.

Thank you for being here, for wanting to do things differently, thank you, thank you, thank you. With love, always.

Mama Nicole

The eight disciplines of the dragon

- Look Inside Yourself

- Look Around You

- Change Your Perspective

- Manage Your Wealth

- Sow in Every Season

- Provoke the Universe

- Improve the Improvement

- Tiger, Snake, Rabbit

Justknow The eight disciplines of the dragon

Daily strategies to work your SUCCESS

+INFO

http:// www.theeightdisciplinesofthedragon.justknow.es

Authors for Training

Editatum and Justknow connect you with your favorite authors to offer you our training service.

Talks, conferences, and practical courses for your organization's events and training.

Leading authors with great communication skills, sense of humor, and ability to surprise the auditorium with practical analysis, advice and key points to drive him in every one of their presentations.

Conferences, talks and courses that offer an entertaining learning process in many diverse fields and topics, designed to satisfy anyone's urge to learn.

Consult our extensive offering at:

www.editatumconferencias.com

And organize relevant events for your attendees with the best professionals in each subject.

Our Collections

Knowledge & Culture

Guides for anyone who wants to expand their knowledge on specific subjects: major historical figures, periods, cultures, religions, etc., offering the reader a broad and rich view of each topic, in language that is accessible to everyone.

Business & Finance

Guides to successfully manage a business, sell a product, service or cause, or become an entrepreneur. Guidelines to lead a work team, create a marketing campaign, or develop the right leadership style, etc.

Science & Technology

Guides to optimize technology, learn to write a great blog, get the most out of your mobile phone. Tips for good SEO positioning, client capture via Facebook, Twitter, Instagram, etc.

Personal Growth

Guides for growth. How to create a quality blog, get a promotion, or develop your communication skills. Tools to stay motivated, teach you how to say "no", or discover the keys to success, etc.

Health & Wellbeing

Practical guides for health and wellbeing. How to manage your time better, how to unwind, or how to lose weight while eating at work. Strategies to stay young, present the best version of yourself, and maintain your physical and mental health, etc.

Home & Family

Practical guides for domestic life. Tips to prevent cyberbullying, create an urban garden, or manage your emotions. Guidelines to decorate by recycling, cooking for events, keeping your children entertained, etc.

Leisure & Free Time

Practical guides for any activity that isn't work or a basic house chore. Games, traveling... in short, hobbies that allow you to enjoy your free time.

Sport & Physical Activity

Guides to learn or prefect your technique in sports or physical activities written by the best professionals in the simplest, most instructional way possible.

www.ingramcontent.com/pod-product-compliance
Lightning Source LLC
LaVergne TN
LVHW090010180726

843489LV00001B/472